THE *TERFINNAS* AND *BEORMAS* OF OHTHERE

BY

ALAN S. C. ROSS

REPRINTED
WITH AN ADDITIONAL NOTE BY
THE AUTHOR

AND AN AFTERWORD BY
MICHAEL CHESNUTT

VIKING SOCIETY FOR NORTHERN RESEARCH
UNIVERSITY COLLEGE LONDON
1981

Made and printed in Great Britain by
TITUS WILSON AND SON LTD., KENDAL

© 1981 Viking Society for Northern Research

This work was originally published in 1940 as Leeds School of English Language Texts and Monographs 7. The Russian and Finnish Summaries that were issued with that edition are not included in the present reprint, the map has been re-drawn, and an Afterword has been added. Publication of this volume has been made possible by a gift to the University of Cambridge in memory of Dorothea Coke, Skjaeret, 1951.

ISBN 0 903521 14 8

CONTENTS

PREFACE TO THE FIRST EDITION	5
PREFACE TO THE SECOND EDITION	9
ABBREVIATIONS	11
OHTHERE'S "NORTHERN" VOYAGE	15
THE *TERFINNAS*	24
THE *BEORMAS*	
I Evidence	29
II Identification	42
III Russian *Perm'*	59
IV The Muslim sources	59
ADDITIONAL NOTE (1940)	62
ADDITIONAL NOTE (1978): BJARMIAN NAMES IN LITERARY TRADITION	64
AFTERWORD	66
SELECT BIBLIOGRAPHY AND ABBREVIATED REFERENCES	83
MAP	at end

If any man shoulde haue take*n* this voiage [*sc.* Ochther's] in hand, by the incouragment of this onely author, he should haue beene thought but simple: consideringe that this Nauigation was writte*n* so many yeares past, in so barbarous a tongue by one onely obscure author, and yet wee in these our dayes finde by our owne experiences, his former reports to be true.

                       Sir Humfrey Gilbert,
*   A Discovrse Of a Discouerie
            for a new Passage to Cataia.*

PREFACE TO THE FIRST EDITION

Ohthere's Voyage is one of the best known passages in Old English literature and it finds a place in most Old English readers. It presents many acutely difficult problems of historical geography, of which the present monograph deals with two—the identification of the *Terfinnas* and the *Beormas*. On these two points the student in England or America receives little help of any value. I take two examples by way of illustration.

I made the acquaintance of this text when a student (some twelve years ago) in the Honours School of English Language at Oxford. We read this text in H. Sweet, *An Anglo-Saxon Reader* (9th ed., 1922)[1]—perhaps the best known Anglo-Saxon reader in England—and for Ohthere's Voyage we were also advised to make use of the annotated map entitled "*The Ninth Century Voyages of Ohthere & Wulfstan*" by J. Keays-Young (published by Basil Blackwell, Oxford, 1926).

On the points under consideration these sources give the following information. Miss Keays-Young says "*Finnas*. The Finns lived in the extreme north of Norway" and Sweet glosses *Finnas* (*Glossary*, s.v.) by 'Fins' (*sic*). Under *Terfinnaland* Miss Keays-Young says "This stretched from the Northern part of the Gulf of Bothnia to the North Cape," though on her map she marks the *Terfinnas* only as occupying the north coast of the Kola Peninsula. In his note to 1.29 (p. 206) Sweet says "*Beormas*, Permians" (which, since no undergraduate can reasonably be expected to have heard of the *Permjaki*, does not convey what he intended). Miss Keays-Young also takes the *Beormas* as "Permians"; she says that the river reached by Ohthere was probably the Dvina and, on her map, places his *Beormas* across the Dvina and Mezen'.

If a recent Anglo-Saxon reader[1a] which I have before me is a fair sample, the same type of information is supplied to

---
[1] Which, owing to circumstances beyond the reviser's control, differed little from the 8th.
[1a] G. P. Krapp and A. G. Kennedy, *An Anglo-Saxon Reader* (New York, 1929).

the American student also. The editors quote from K. Gjerset's *History of the Norwegian People* (New York, 1915):—"'Ohthere . . . gave the English king . . . an account of . . . . . his exploration of Finland and Bjarmeland (the land of the Permians) ' (Gjerset i, 142) " [note to 40.1]. They add [note to 41.2]:—" The name *Terfinn* as a name for the Finns has not survived, is recorded nowhere else . . . In modern use, the term Finns also includes the Lapps."

Of this information it will suffice to say here that it is totally at variance with the views which have obtained for nearly a century in the abundant specialist literature of the subject. The historical geography of Ohthere's Voyage (and particularly of the two peoples considered here) has naturally always been of the greatest interest to the Finno-Ugrist, since it is one of the earliest and most valuable sources in a subject notably lacking in such sources. There is consequently an extensive literature on the subject, mostly in Finnish but partly in Russian and the Scandinavian languages, going back almost a hundred years.[2] Much of this literature is not accessible in England.

That the English and American writers quoted above are unfamiliar with the Finnish and Russian literature is not perhaps surprising, but the fact that they have not consulted either such classic articles in the Scandinavian languages as Storm's (see p. 24), or Vasmer's excellent paper on the *Terfinnas*, which appeared in German (*Englische Studien* lvi, 169-71), can hardly be condoned.[3]

The conclusions which I reach in the present monograph may be summarised as follows. The *Terfinnas* must be located on Kandalaks Bay, not in the Dvina area.

[2] Thus the *Beormas* seem first to have been identified as Karelians (see p. 49) by M. A. Castrén in his " Anmärkningar om Savolotschesskaja Tschud " (*Suomi* 1844, pp. 1-22) and the *Terfinnas*' connection with the Terskij Bereg was first made clear by J. A. Sjögren (see p. 25).

[3] It is pleasant to be able to record two exceptions to this criticism of the English and American scholarship on the point; I refer to the striking article of K. Malone " King Alfred's North: A study in mediaeval geography " (*Speculum* v, 139-67) and the very brief but accurate notes in A. J. Wyatt, *An Anglo-Saxon Reader*, Note to II.81; *Index of Persons and Places* s.v. *Beormas*.

This follows *a*) from Ohthere's Log and *b*) from the geographical distribution of the name *Ter*; they may in fact be identified with the Lapps of the Terskij Bereg. *Bjarmaland*, the country of the OWN. *Bjarmar* (Ohthere's *Beormas*) was divided into two parts, *Biarmia ulterior* and *Biarmia citerior*. We may locate the former in the Dvina area (for the river is frequently mentioned) and the latter, the country of Ohthere's *Beormas*, on Kandalaks Bay (for it adjoined the land of the *Terfinnas*). The *Beormas-Bjarmar* have been considered, in turn, as Lapps, as Komi and as Baltic Fenns— either Vatja, Veps or Karelians. But the evidence afforded by the name of the god of the *Bjarmar*, OWN. *Jomali* (cf. Finn. *jumala* ' god ') and Ohthere's statement that the Lapps (*Terfinnas*) and the *Beormas* spoke almost the same language, considered in the light of the historical data, show that the *Beormas* can only have been Baltic Fenns, in all probability Karelians. In LSE vi, 5-13 I further argue that the word *Bjarmar* is probably of Germanic origin (cf. MnE. *brim*, etc.); it passed from OWN. into Old Northern Karelian (with change of initial *b* to *p*), thence into Russian, giving ORuss. *Per(e)mъ* (MnRuss. *Perm'*).

I should like to have dealt with the Russian side of the question more fully, but this has unfortunately proved impossible. By making use of the combined resources of all the large libraries in England the study of Finno-Ugrian philology is just possible,[4] but any exhaustive study of Slavonic philology here would appear to be very difficult for more than half the essential books (both pre- and post-War) are not available. There is a large and important Russian literature on the *Perm'*-question but I have here merely attempted the briefest of summaries.[5]

[4] Even so many essential books are lacking in this country. I may mention E. N. Setälä's *Yhteissuomalainen äännehistoria* [Gemeinfinnische Lautlehre] and the dissertations (both pre- and post-War) of Hungarian universities other than Budapest. Most of the extensive philological literature of post-War Estonia is missing and, finally, next to nothing is to be found of the important descriptive philological literature of the U.S.S.R.

[5] Smirnov's *Permjaki* (of which there is no copy in any English library) contains a valuable collection of Russian references.

The Sketch-Map has been duplicated by means of the Ormig Duplicator. The material for the Finno-Ugrian peoples has been taken from the maps in *Suomen Suku*, vol. ii (at end, and at p. 291); for the Samoyedes Z. E. Chernjakov's *Karta rasprostranenija jazykov narodov Severa SSSR* [A map of the distribution of the languages of the peoples of the North of the U.S.S.R.] (1934) has been used; in addition certain of the entries in Vasmer IV, Map to face p. 270, have been incorporated (see p. 52). I take this opportunity of expressing my gratitude to Mr. Arthur Davies of the Geography Department for the valuable assistance he has given me in the preparation of this map and with various geographical questions; also to Mrs. Cartwright of the Economics Department for the great care she has given to the reproduction of the map.

There remains the pleasant duty of expressing my thanks to the many people who have helped me on various points connected with the present research. First, to Professor Bruce Dickins and E. S. Olszewska for advice on the most diverse points. Further to:—Mr. A. Ph. Anisimov (Institut Narodov Severa, Leningrad); Professor H. W. Bailey (Cambridge); Dr. S. Blöndal (Kongelige Bibliotek, Copenhagen); Mr. S. Burr (Leeds); Mrs. N. K. Chadwick (Cambridge); Dr. V. Kiparsky (Riga); Professor V. Minorsky (School of Oriental Studies, London); Professor J. Percival (Reading); Dr. S. Potter (Southampton); Professor P. Ravila (Turku); Professor P. Savitskij (Prague); Professor M. Schlauch (New York); Mrs. Alette Schreiner (Oslo); Mr. H. Sumner (Balliol College, Oxford); Dr. E. Ó. Sveinsson (Reykjavik); Mr. E. O. G. Turville-Petre; Professor O. J. Tuulio-Tallgren (Helsinki); Dr. C. E. Wright (British Museum).

ALAN S. C. ROSS.

Leeds and Helsinki
1934-39.

PREFACE TO THE SECOND EDITION

This new edition of Professor Ross's monograph contains an unaltered reprint of the original preface and text, including the additional note appended to the first edition (pp. 62-3). A further additional note by the author appears on pp. 64-5. It is followed by an Afterword in which the present writer reviews the conclusions arrived at in the monograph in the light of more recent research, including articles published by Ross himself in the period down to 1954. This was prepared with Professor Ross's active cooperation and I now dedicate it to his memory. He died on 23 September 1980.

A new map prepared by Mr K. Wass, Superintendent of the Drawing Office, Geography Department, University College London, has been substituted for the duplicated sketch-map which accompanied the first edition (cf. p. 8 above). The colouring of the original map has been replaced by varieties of shading, but in all other respects (including the representation of the Finnish-Soviet border) the model of the original has been followed.

Professor Peter Foote and Mr Anthony Faulkes have acted as General Editors of the volume. The Viking Society is especially grateful to Mr Peter Meredith, Editor of Leeds Studies in English, for his ready interest in promoting the publication of this reprint.

Ross's monograph is a remarkable product of the tradition of comparative philology and a testimony to the breadth of its author's interdisciplinary interests, particularly in the area of Finno-Ugric languages and culture. The arrangement here adopted will permit new readers to form an undisturbed impression of the work as it first appeared in 1940. The supplementary matter is intended to provide the more advanced student with a convenient point of departure for further investigation.

MICHAEL CHESNUTT

Copenhagen
April-December 1980

ABBREVIATIONS

I. Names of Languages

[The abbreviations M (Middle), Mn (Modern), O (Old), Pr (Primitive) are used before the names of languages].

BF.	Baltic Fennic[5a]	Kar.	Karelian
Du.	Dutch	Lapp.	Lappish
E.	English	Lat.	Latin
Est.	Estonian	LG.	Low German
Finn.	Finnish	N.	Norse
Fris.	Frisian	Russ.	Russian
Goth.	Gothic	WN.	West Norse
HG.	High German	WS.	West Saxon
Icel.	Icelandic		

II. Names of books, periodicals and articles.

BN = J. Brøndum-Nielsen, *Gammeldansk Grammatik*. Vols. 1-3. Copenhagen. 1928-35.

Bósas. = Bósasaga (see p. 34).

Bósas.[2] = Bósasaga, later version (see p. 35).

Eg.s. = Egilssaga Skallagrímssonar (see p. 31).

Flat. = Flateyjarbók (see p. 32).

FUF = *Finnisch-ugrische Forschungen*.

Hálfss. = Hálfssaga ok Hálfsrekka (see p. 35).

Hfds.Br. = Hálfdanarsaga Brǫnufóstra (see p. 35).

Hfds.Ey. = Hálfdanarsaga Eysteinssonar (see p. 35).

Hist.N. = Historia Norwegiæ (see p. 41).

Hkr. = Heimskringla (see p. 29).

[5a] See LSE ii, 6; it may be noted here that the names of the other Finno-Ugrian languages are those suggested as standard for English LSE iii, 58.

Jaakkola = J. Jaakkola, *Suomen varhaishistoria* [The early history of Finland]. Helsinki. 1935.
Johnsen = O. A. Johnsen, *Finmarkens politiske historie aktmæssig fremstillet*. Kristiania. 1923.
Jónsson = F. Jónsson, *Den norsk-islandske skjaldedigtning*. 4 vols. Copenhagen 1912-15.
Langebek = J. Langebek, *Scriptores Rerum Danicarum Medii Ævi*. 9 vols. Copenhagen. 1772-1878.
Ld.fr. = Landafræði (see p. 39).
LSE = *Leeds Studies in English and Kindred Languages*.
Malone = K. Malone, King Alfred's North: A study in mediaeval geography, *Speculum* v, 139-67.
NED = J. A. H. Murray, etc., *A New English Dictionary*. Oxford. 1884-1928.
Qr.Os. = Qrvar-Oddssaga (see p. 37).
Rafn = C. C. Rafn, *Fornaldar sögur Norðrlanda*. 3 vols. Copenhagen. 1829-30.
SS = *Suomen Suku* [The Finnish Race]. Vols. 1-3. Helsinki. 1926-34.
Sts.st. = Sturlaugssaga Starfsama (see p. 35).
SUSA = *Suomalais- ugrilaisen Seuran Aikakauskirja* [*Journal de la Société Finno-ougrienne*].
SUST = *Suomalais- ugrilaisen Seuran Toimituksia* [= *Mémoires* . . .].
Tallgren = A. M. Tallgren, Biarmia, *Eurasia Septentrionalis Antiqua* vi, 99-120.
Tiander = K. Tiander, *Poezdki Skandinavov v Beloe More* [The voyages of the Scandinavians to the White Sea]. St Petersburg. 1906.
Uotila = T. E. Uotila, *Zur geschichte des konsonantismus in den permischen sprachen* (SUST 65).
Uotila *Vir.* = . . . , Huomautuksia syrjäänin itämerensuomalaisista lainasanoista [Notes on the Baltic Fennic loan-words of Komi], *Virittäjä* 1936, pp. 199-208.
Vasmer *ESt* = M. Vasmer, Zum namen der Terfinnas in König Ælfreds Orosius-übersetzung, *Englische Studien* lvi, 169-71.

Vasmer II = . . . , Beiträge zur historischen Völkerkunde Osteuropas: II. Die ehemalige Ausbreitung der Westfinnen in den heutigen slavischen Ländern, *Sitzungsberichte der Preussischen Akademie der Wissenschaften* 1934, *Philosophisch-historische Klasse* pp. 351-440.

Vasmer IV = . . . , . . . : IV. Die ehemalige Ausbreitung der Lappen und Permier in Nordrussland, *ibid.* 1936, *Philosophisch-historische Klasse* pp. 176-270.

Wichmann = Y. Wichmann, Syrjäänit ja karjalaiset [Komi and Karelians], *Valvoja* 1920 pp. 400-09.

Wiklund = K. B. Wiklund, *Entwurf einer urlappischen lautlehre* I (SUST 10.i).

WP = A. Walde and J. Pokorny, *Vergleichendes Wörterbuch der indogermanischen Sprachen.* 3 vols. Berlin. 1930-2.

OHTHERE'S "NORTHERN" VOYAGE

I give the text from the two manuscripts, the Lauderdale MS. (*L*) above and MS. Cotton Tiberius B.1 (*C*)[6] below. The Lauderdale Manuscript belongs to Lord Tollemache, of Helmingham Hall, Suffolk. I regret to say that this manuscript has not been made accessible to me. But Dr. S. Potter (Southampton), who has recently collated it, kindly informs me that Sweet's text of the passage printed here is accurate. The details of the capitalisation and paragraphing (points in which Sweet does not follow the manuscript) are taken from the facsimile of this section of the Lauderdale MS. given by J. Bosworth, *King Alfred's Anglo-Saxon Version of the Compendious History of the World by Orosius*, Plates to face p. 18, which is doubtless sufficiently accurate for this purpose. (I follow Sweet's paragraphing in the translation). There is a gap in *L* at the word *hyd* which extends beyond the end of our excerpt. In both MSS. I follow H. Sweet (*King Alfred's Orosius* pp. 17-18) as to punctuation but the manuscripts as to capitalisation and paragraphing. In the part for which I print both MSS. I obelise an erroneous form (or space for a word erroneously omitted) in the one text which is correct in the other.

---

[6] Both the *Orosius* and the *Chronicle* sections of this manuscript have been annotated—in the margins and between the lines—by Robert Talbot (d. 1558—see *Dictionary of National Biography* s.n.); see J. Earle and C. Plummer, *Two of the Saxon Chronicles parallel* ii, p. xxxi.

16   THE *TERFINNAS* & *BEORMAS* OF OHTHERE

p.13   *L* ohthere sæde his hlaforde, ælfrede cyninge, þæt he
ealra norðmonna norþmest bude. he cwæð þæt he bude on
þæm lande norþweardum wiþ þa westsǽ. he sæde þeah
þæt † land sie swiþe lang norþ þonan; ac hit is eal weste,
buton on feawum stowum styccemælum wiciað finnas, on
huntoðe on wintra, 7 on sumera on fiscaþe be þære sǽ. he
sæde þæt he æt sumum cirre wolde fandian hu longe þæt
land norþryhte læge, oþþe hwæðer ænig mon be norðan þæm
westenne bude. þa for he norþryhte be þæm lande: let
p.14 him ealne weg / þæt weste land on ðæt steorbord, 7 þa widsæ
on ðæt bæcbord þrie dagas. þa wæs he swa feor norþ swa
þa hwælhuntan firrest faraþ. þa for he þagiet norþryhte swa
feor swa he meahte on þæm oþrum þrim dagum gesiglan.
þa beag þæt land þær eastryhte, oþþe seo sǽ in on ðæt lond,
he nysse hwæðer; buton he wisse ðæt he ðær bád westanwindes 7 hwon norþan, 7 siglde ða east be lande swa swa he
meahte on feower dagum gesiglan. þa sceolde he ðær bidan

f.11.v.   *C* Ohthere sæde his hlaforde, ælfrede kynincge, þæt he
ealra norðmanna norðmest bude. he cwæð þæt he bude on
þæm lande norðeweardum wið ða westsǽ. hé sæde ðeah
þæt þæt land sy swyðe lang norð þanon; ac hit is eall weste,
buton on feawum stowum sticcemælum wiciað finnas, on
huntaðe on wintra, 7 on sumera on fiscnoðe[11] be ðære sǽ. hé
sæde þæt he æt sumum cyrre wolde fandian hú lange þæt
land norðrihte læge, oððe hwæþer ænig man be norðan þæm
westene bude. þa fór hé norðrihte be þæm lande: lét hím
ealne weg þæt weste land on þæt steorbord, 7 þa widsǽ on
bæcbord þry dagas. þa wæs he swa feor[12] norð swa þa
hwælhuntan fyrrest farað. þa fór he þagyt norðryhte swa
hé mihte on þæm oþrum þrim dagum geseglian. ða beah
þæt land þær eastryhte, oððe sio sǽ in on þæt land, he nyste
hwæþer; buton he wiste þæt he þær abad[13] westanwindes
f.12.r. †oððe hwón/norðan, 7 seglede þanon east be lande swa swa
hé mihte on feower dagum geseglian. þa sceolde he abidan[14]

[11] *Altered from* fiscoðe.
[12] *A second* r *erased here.*
[13] *Altered from* bad.
[14] *Altered from* bidan.

THE *TERFINNAS* & *BEORMAS* OF OHTHERE 17

Ohthere told his lord, King Alfred, that he dwelt[16a] furthest north of all Norwegians.[17] He said that he dwelt in the north of that country on the coast of the Norwegian Sea.[18] He said however that that country extended very far to the north[19] from where he lived; but it is all uninhabited[20] except that, in a few places, here and there, Lapps are encamped, hunting in winter and, in summer, fishing in the sea.

He said that once he wished to ascertain how far the land extended due north, or whether anyone lived to the north of the uninhabited land. So he went due north along the coast; he kept, for three days, the uninhabited land to starboard and the open sea to port, all the way. Then he was as far north as the whalers go at their furthest. Then he went on—still due north—as far as he could sail in the next three days. Then the land curved away due east (or the sea entered the land—he did not know which of the two);[21] he only knew that there he waited for a westerly wind with a touch of north in it; and he then[22] sailed east along the coast as far as he could sail in four days. There[23] he had to

---

[16a] Ohthere's home is usually put on the Malangen Fjord or thereabouts (Malone p. 158), but was more probably somewhat further north (Johnsen p. 7).
[17] *Norðmenn* ' Norwegians ' (Malone p. 157).
[18] *West-sæ* ' North Sea and also Norwegian Sea ' (Malone p. 157).
[19] Malone uses his theory that Alfred's compass-points are shifted 45° clockwise out of the true to explain Ohthere's *norþ* for the actual north-east, etc. (p. 158). But I do not follow Malone in the translation on this point.
[20] *wēste*; see pp. 44-5.
[21] i.e. he did not know whether he was rounding an extreme point or entering a large gulf.
[22] *C* : thence.
[23] There; *L only*.

ryhtnorþanwindes, for ðæm þæt land beag þær suþryhte,
oþþe seo sǽ in on ðæt land, he nysse hwæþer. þa siglde he
þonan suðryhte be lande swa swa he mehte on fíf dagum
gesiglan. ða læg þær an micel ea up in on þæt land. þa
cirdon hie up in on ða⁷ ea, for þæm hie ne dorston forþ bi
þære ea siglan for unfriþe; for þæm ðæt land wæs eall gebun
on oþre healfe þære eas. ne mette he ær nán gebun land,
siþþan he from his agnum hám fór. Ac him wæs ealne weg
weste land on þæt steorbord, butan fiscerum 7 fugelerum
7 huntum, 7 þæt wæron eall finnas; 7 him wæs á widsǽ on
ðæt bæcbord. þa beormas⁸ hæfdon swiþe wel gebúd hira
land; Ac hie ne dorston þær on cuman. Ac þara terfinna
land wæs eal weste buton † huntan gewicodon, oþþe fisceras,
oþþe †fugelas. fela spella him sædon þa beormas⁹ ægþer
ge of hiera agnum lande ge of þæm landum þe ymb hie utan
wæron; Ac he nyste hwæt þæs soþes wæs, for þæm he hit
self ne geseah.¹⁰ þa finnas, him þuhte, 7 þa beormas⁸

⁷ *Erasure after* a (= ðam ?).
⁸ *First stroke of the* m *erased.*
⁹ *Last stroke of the* m *erased.*
¹⁰ *No stop in Sweet's text.*

ryhtenorðanwindes, for ðan þæt land þær beah suðrihte,
oððe seo sæ in on þæt land, he nyste hwæþer. ða seglede
he þanon suðrihte be lande swa swa he mihte on fif dagum
geseglian. þa læg þær án mycel ea úp in *þæt* land. þa
cyrdon hý up in on ða ea, for þæm hy ne dorston forð be
þære éa seglian for unfriðe; for ðæm þæt land wæs eall
gebún on oðre healfe þære éa. ne mette he ǽr nán gebún
land, syððan he fram hys agnum hame fór. Ac him wæs ealne
weg weste land on þæt steorbord, butan fisceran 7 fugeleran
7 huntan, 7 þæt wæran ealle finnas; 7 him wæs á wídsǽ
on þæt bæcbord. ða beormas hæfdon swiðe well gebún hyra
land; Ac hi ne dorston þær on cuman. Ac ðara terfinna land
wæs eall weste butan þær húntan gewicodon, oððe fisceras,
oððe fugeleras. fela spella him sædon ða beormas ægþer ge
of hyra agenum lande ge of þæm †lande þe ymb hý utan
wæran; Ac he nyste hwæt þæs soðes wæs, for ðæm hé hít
sylf ne geseah. þa finnas, him þuhte, 7 þa beormas spræcon

THE *TERFINNAS* & *BEORMAS* OF OHTHERE

wait for a due north wind because the land curved away there due south (or the sea entered the land—he did not know which of the two).[21] Then he sailed thence due south along the coast as far as he could sail in five days. There a great river went up into the land. Then they turned up into the river, because they dared not sail on past the river for fear of hostilities; because, on the other side of the river, the land was thoroughly cultivated. Before this he had not met with any cultivated land, since he had left his own home; but, all the way, he had had uninhabited land to starboard (except for fishers and fowlers and hunters—and these had all been Lapps) and, to port, always open sea. The Beormas[24] had cultivated their land very well; but they did not dare go ashore there. But the land of the Terfinnas was entirely uninhabited except where hunters or fishers or fowlers were encamped.[25]

The Beormas[26] told him many tales, both of their own country, and also of the countries which were round about them; but, as to these, he did not know what was truth in them, because he had not seen for himself. It seemed to him that the Lapps and the Beormas spoke almost the

---

[24] In *L* the unfamiliar word *Beormas* has, in each case, been altered (by erasure) to the familiar *beornas* ' men.'

[25] See pp. 44-5.

[26] There is a discrepancy here: Ohthere did not dare set foot on the territory of the Beormas and yet " they told him many tales." The most probable solution would appear to be that Ohthere landed at an up-river settlement of Terfinnas on their frontier (cf. p. 58) with the Beormas to which, doubtless for reasons of trade (cf. p. 46), the latter were in the habit of coming peacefully.

spræcon neah an geþeode. swiþost he for ðider, toeacan
þæs landes sceawunge, for þæm horschwælum, for ðæm hie
habbað swiþe æþele bán on hiora toþum—þa teð hie brohton
sume þæm cyninge —, 7 hiora hyd

neah án geðeode Swiðost he fór ðyder, toeacan þæs landes
sceawunge, for ðæm horshwælum, for ðæm hý[15] habbað swyðe
æþele bán on hyra toþum—þa teð hy brohton sume þæm
f.12.v. cynincge—,/7 hyra hýd bið swiðe gód to scíprapum. se
hwǽl bið micle læssa þonne oðre hwalas: ne bið hé lengra
ðonne syfan elna lang. ac on his agnum lande is se betsta
hwælhuntað: þa beoð eahta and feowertiges elna lange, 7
þa mæstan fíftiges elna lange. þara hé sæde þæt he syxa
sum ofsloge syxtig on twam dagum. hé wæs swyðe spedig
man on þæm æhtum þe heora speda on beoð, þæt is, on
wildeorum.[16] he hæfde þagyt, ða hé þone cyningc sohte,
tamra deora unbebohtra syx hund. þa deor hý[15] hátað
'hránas'; þara wæron syx stælhranas; ða beoð swyðe dyre
mid finnum, for ðæm hy foð þa wildan hranas mid. he wæs
mid þæm fyrstum mannum on þæm lande: Næfde he þeah
ma ðonne twentig hryðera, 7 twentig sceapa, 7 twentig
swyna; 7 þæt lytle þæt he erede he erede mid horsan. Ac
hyra ár is mæst on þæm gafole þe ða finnas him gyldað.
þæt gafol bið on deora fellum, 7 on fugela feðerum, 7 hwales
bane, 7 on þæm sciprapum, þe beoð of hwæles hyde geworht,
7 of seoles. Æghwilc gylt be hys gebyrdum. se byrdesta
sceall gyldan fiftyne mearðes fell, 7 fíf hranes, 7 an beran
fel, 7 tyn ambra feðra, 7 berenne kyrtel oððe yterenne, 7
twegen scíprapas; ægþer sý syxtig elna lang, oþer sy of
hwæles hýde geworht, oþer of sioles. hé sæde ðæt norðmanna
f.13.r. land wære swyþe lang 7 swyðe/smæl. eal þæt hís man aþer
oððe ettan oððe erian mæg þæt lið wið ða sǽ; 7 þæt is þeah
on sumum stowum swyðe cludig; 7 licgað wilde moras wið

[15] *Altered from* í. [16] *Altered from* wildrum.

same language. Apart from the exploring of the country, he went there principally for the walruses, for they have very fine bone in their tusks (they brought some of the tusks to the king) and their hide // is very good for ships' cables. This kind of 'whale'[27] is much smaller than other whales; it is not longer than seven ells. But in his [Ohthere's] own country is the best whaling; those [whales] are forty-eight ells long, the largest, fifty. He said that, with five companions, he had slain sixty of these in two days.

He was a very rich man in the kind of property in which their wealth consists, namely, in wild animals. At the time he visited the king he still had six hundred tame beasts unsold; these animals they call 'reindeer'; among them were six decoy-reindeer; these are very valuable among the Lapps, because with them they catch the wild reindeer. He [Ohthere] was among the principal men of the country; he had, however, no more than twenty head of cattle, twenty sheep and twenty pigs; and the little that he ploughed he ploughed with horses. But their wealth consists mostly of the tribute which the Lapps pay them. This tribute consists of skins of animals, of birds' down, of whalebone, and of the cables which are made of whale-hide and seal-skin. Everyone pays according to his rank. A man of the highest rank must pay fifteen martens' skins, five reindeer-hides, one bear-skin, ten measures of down, a kirtle made of bear- or otter-skin, and two ships' cables (both to be sixty ells long, one made of whale-hide and the other of seal-skin).

He said that the country of the Norwegians was very long and very narrow. All of it that can be grazed or ploughed lies by the sea; but even this is very rocky in some places. And wild mountains[28] lie to the east, parallel with and above

---

[27] i.e. the walrus.
[28] *mōras*; the geographical context clearly indicates 'mountains' as the meaning of this word—rather than 'waste ground' (NED. s.v. *Moor.* sb.¹1); the required sense is found elsewhere in Old English; cf. Lindisfarne Gospels *mor* 'mons,' *passim.*

22 THE *TERFINNAS* & *BEORMAS* OF OHTHERE

eastan 7 wið uppon emnlange þæm bynum lande. On þæm morum eardiað finnas. 7 þæt byne land is easteweard bradost, 7 symle swa norðor swa smælre. eastewerd hit mæg bion syxtig mila brad, oþþe hwene brædre; 7 middeweard þritig oððe bradre; 7 norðeweard he cwæð, þær hit smalost være, *þæt* hit mihte beon þreora mila brad to þæm more; 7 se mór syðþan, on sumum stowum, swa brad swa man mæg on twam wucum oferferan; 7 on sumum stowum swa brad swa man mæg on syx dagum oferferan. ðonne is toemnes þæm lande suðeweardum, on oðre healfe þæs mores, sweoland, oþ þæt land norðeweard; 7 toemnes þæm lande norðeweardum cwenaland. þa cwenas hergiað hwilum on ða norðmen ofer ðone mor, hwilum þa norðmen on hy. 7 þær sint swiðe micle meras fersce geond þa moras; 7 berað þa cwenas hyra scypu ofer land on ða meras, 7 þanon hergiað on ða norðmen; hy habbað swyðe lytle scypa 7 swyðe leohte. Ohthere sæde *þæt* sio scír hatte halgoland þe hé on bude. he cwæð þæt nán man ne bude be norðan him.

the cultivated land.[29] On these mountains dwell Lapps. And the cultivated land is widest in the south[30]; and, always, the further north you go the narrower it becomes. In the south it may be sixty miles wide, or a little wider; in the middle, thirty or more; and, in the north where it was narrowest, he said that it might be three miles across to the mountains; after this the mountains are, in some places, as wide as can be traversed in a fortnight, and, in others, as wide as can be traversed in six days.

On the other side of the mountains, parallel to the south part of the country, there is Sweden;[31] parallel to the north part, Cwena-land.[32] The Cwenas sometimes make attacks on the Norwegians across the mountains, at other times the Norwegians attack them. Throughout the mountains there are very large fresh-water lakes; the Cwenas carry their boats overland to these lakes, and from there they attack the Norwegians; they have very small and light boats.

Ohthere said that the district in which he lived was called " Helgeland." He said that no one dwelt north of him.

---

[29] See pp. 44-5.
[30] *easteweard* ' south ' (Malone p. 159; J. Fritzner, *Ordbog over det gamle norske Sprog* s.v. *austr* adv.).
[31] *Swēoland* ' Sweden ' (Malone p. 159).
[32] See p. 24, note 4.

THE *TERFINNAS*

Since the publication of G. Storm's classic lecture " Om opdagelsen af ' Nordkap ' og veien til 'det hvide hav' " (given 24/1/1894)[1] the general outlines of this part of Ohthere's geography have not been in dispute. It is clear that he reached the White Sea. But the ' great river ' up which he went cannot be the Dvina;[2] it must be one of the rivers flowing south into Kandalaks Bay; it may be the Varzuga, the Umba or, conceivably, the head of the Bay itself (see Johnsen p. 9).[3] Two facts attest this:—first, Ohthere's definite statement that, during his entire journey to this river, he had always had land to starboard and open sea to port—which shows that he must have sailed along the *West* coast of the White Sea, not the East; secondly, his reference to the *Ter-finnas*.

No good purpose will be served here by discussing the history of the word *Finn*[4] in detail; it is quite well-known. Suffice it to say that, in our early sources, the word (Greek

[1] *Det norske geografiske Selskabs årbog* v, 91-106.

[2] This view (see p. 5) is merely due to the presence of Bjarmar on the Dvina (see p. 43).

[3] Ohthere's statement " they turned up into the river, because they dared not sail on past the river " is in favour of the identification of the river as either the Varzuga or the Umba, rather than as the head of the Bay. For " to sail on past " the latter would have involved a complete reversal of the course; Ohthere can hardly have meant this by " sailing on past " and, if he had been so far up the Bay that he thought it was a river, he would have been able to see across it and must therefore have been aware that a reversal of the course would have been necessary. Of the two rivers—the Varzuga or the Umba—it is tempting to prefer the former in view of the ' Karelian parishes ' mentioned in this area in 1419 (see p. 56) and of the find at its mouth (Tallgren Fig. 1, No. 12).

[4] For, as its title implies, this monograph is concerned only with the *Terfinnas* and the *Beormas*. I therefore also refrain from any discussion of the Cwenas. These (: OWN. *Kvenir*) present one of the best-known problems of Finnish history, a problem associated with many of the great names of Finno-Ugrian philology. Here it will be sufficient to say that—despite philological (see LSE. v, 101) and other difficulties—they may be the same as the Suomi-Finnish *Kainulaiset* and that, in any case, they are to be considered as a northern Suomi-Finnish tribe. For further information the reader is referred to two standard works on the question:— J. Laurosela, *Kveen-kainulais-kysymys* [The Cwēn-Kainulaiset question] (*Historiallinen Arkisto* xxii) and K. Grotenfelt, *Über die alten kvänen und Kvänland* (*Annales Academiæ Scientiarum Fennicæ* B.I.i); see also Jaakkola pp. 332-53.

Φίννοι Lat. *Fenni, Finni*⁵ ON. *Finnar*—whence Ohthere's *Finnas*) is used with reference to two different peoples *viz*. the Lapps and the Baltic Fenns (particularly, in its modern sense, to the Suomi-Finns) and that Ohthere's *Finnas* are certainly Lapps, not Finns.⁶ The *Terfinnas* must therefore be a particular group of Lapps. That they are the Lapps of the modern Russian *Terskij bereg* ' south-east coast of the Kola Peninsula '⁷ is an obvious suggestion which appears as early as J. A. Sjögren (cf. his *Gesammelte Schriften* i, 349 note 396). In a valuable article in *Englische Studien* (lvi, 169-71) M. Vasmer discusses the references to ORuss. *Trě* (whence MnRuss. *Terskij bereg*), the early name for the south coast of the Kola Peninsula. He shows that we may postulate the series *Tbrě > ORuss. *Tbrě* (and cf. ORuss. *Tbrbskbjb beregb*) > ORuss. *Trě, Terě* (XIII-XIV cent.)—hence MnRuss. *Terskij bereg*. In Kola-Lappish the most eastern part of the Kola Peninsula is called *Tarje*.⁸ The use of the name *Turja* in the Finnish folk-poetry (e.g. Kalevala xii. 138, 199; xxvi. 294; xlii. 546; xliii. 336; xlviii. 313) is rendered sufficiently clear by E. Lönnrot's gloss in his *Finskt-svenskt Lexikon* s.v. *Turja*: ' the country on the other side of the mountains in the North; Norway; Lapland '; cf. further his *Turjan meri* ' the Arctic Ocean '. In the Kalevala *Turja* is thought of as adjacent to Lapland and, in the following passage (in which the people of Pohjola—the Kingdom of the North— are seeking a slaughterer for their great ox), its position on the extreme confines of the northern world is clear, for it is placed between Lapland and the Kingdoms of the Dead, Tuonela and Manala:—" They caused a search

⁵ M. Schönfeld, *Wörterbuch der altgermanischen Personen- und Völkernamen* s. vv. *Fenni* (p. 275), *Scrithifinni (p. 279).
⁶ See SS i, 264 ff. If we accept the current etymology of *Finn* as a Germanic word to the IndE. root *pent-* (WP ii, 26-7) closely related to OE. *fundian* ' to hasten ' OHG. *fendo* ' pedestrian ' and assign a meaning such as ' wanderer, nomad ' to it, its application to two totally distinct tribes (cf. p. 59) is readily intelligible.
⁷ More accurately, the coast " stretching from the entrance of the White Sea to the Varzuga River " (E. Rae, *The White Sea Peninsula* p. 29).
⁸ A. Genetz, *Wörterbuch der kola-lappischen Dialekte* p. 185.

to be made for a slaughterer of the great ox, for one who would subdue him—from beautiful Karelia, from the great spaces of Finland, from the gentle[9] land of Russia, from the courageous land of Sweden, from the broad limits of Lapland, from the mighty land of *Turja*; they caused a search to be made for him from Tuonela, from Manala, from the terrestrial depths; they caused a search to be made but he was not found; they caused a search to be made, he was not found " (xx. 73-84).[10]

It is thus clear that the name under discussion here is particularly associated with the Kola Peninsula, though within this area there appears to be some slight variation in the details of its application. Finally it should be noted that there is no trace of the name *east* of the White Sea.

Since at so early a date the Russians can hardly have been in direct contact with the Lapps (see LSE. vi, 6 note 4), Vasmer concludes that the Russian form of the name is derived from a Karelian[11] **Turja* identical with the Finnish form quoted above.[12] The corresponding form in PrLapp. (which will sufficiently represent the ' Terfinnish ' of Ohthere's day) would—according to a letter (22/5/1921) of K. B. Wiklund's quoted by Vasmer—have been **Tįrjā*. The ultimate origin of the name is uncertain, nor can we decide whether *Turja* is a Lappish loan-word in Baltic Fennic, or whether the Lappish and Baltic Fennic words are merely ultimately related.[13]

[9] The word *vieno* ' gentle, peaceful ' applied to Russia in this standard Kalevala phrase is usually considered to be a corruption of *Viena* ' the Dvina '; see E. N. Setälä, SUST XXXV. xiii. 7 ff.

[10] In addition MnFinn. *Turja* is used specifically of a small peninsula on the south coast of the Kola Peninsula—hence its MnRuss. name *Turij* (see Sketch-Map).

[11] See p. 57.

[12] For the development in the second syllable, BF. *ja* > Russ. *e*, Vasmer compares Russ. *Korela* : Finn. *Karjala* ' Karelia ' (for Russ. *o* < BF. *a*, as in Russ. *ol'ga* ' swampy district ' < Finn. *alho*, see J. Kalima, *Die ostseefinnischen Lehnwörter im russischen* p. 46). Initial BF. *ja* appears as *e* (beside *ja*) in Russ. *emega*, *jamega* ' mesh of a weir-basket ' < Kar. *jamo*, *jame* (Finn. *jame*)—see Kalima, *op. cit.* p. 48. The Russian representation may perhaps be due to the change of Russ. *ja* > *e* before ' soft ' consonants in the Northern Russian dialects; cf. Northern Russ. *gres*' ' dirt,' *opet*' ' again ' : standard (i.e. Southern) Russ. *grjaz*', *opjat*' (see K. H. Meyer, *Historische Grammatik der russischen Sprache* i, 14).

[13] For the correspondence between Lappish *į* (i.e., in the more usual orthography,

The phonological position of OE. *Ter-* relative to the Finno-Ugrian forms is of interest. As to the first syllable. It is first of all obvious (as Vasmer *ESt* points out) that the *e* can have no direct connection with that of MnRuss. *Terskij*, since the *e* in the latter form is comparatively recent. Vasmer dismisses the OE. *e* as due to 'zufällige Übereinstimmung' but some further discussion seems desirable. OE. *Ter-* is, of course, really a spoken OWN. form, OWN. **Ter-*. Unless we regard Alfred's *Ter-* as erroneous and emend it to **Tur-* or **Tyr-* (cf. p. 18, note 15)—which would hardly be justifiable—it cannot be considered to represent a BF. **Turja*. But it can well represent a PrLapp. **Târjā*—and this is on other grounds more probable, for while Ohthere probably knew Lappish he was almost certainly ignorant of Bjarmian (see further p. 48). Two suggestions as to the details of this representation might be put forward:—(i) OWN. **Ter-* might well have served as a reasonably accurate 'Lautersatz' for a PrLapp. **Târ-* (with the unfamiliar 'back' *i*) or (ii) if we can assume that the *a*-quality of Modern Kola-Lappish *Tarje* was beginning to appear even at this early date, an original **Tarjā* would naturally appear as **Teria* in OWN.—by reason either of actual *i*-umlaut or of 'positional analogy' with words of similar type (e.g. OIcel. *veria* = Goth. *warjan*).[14]

The second syllable of PrLapp. **Târjā* is not represented in Alfred's *Ter-*. There can of course be no question of a phonological loss of the second syllable in OWN.; the word would fall into line with forms such as OIcel. *fer-ia, sel-ia, ver-ia* with preserved *j*; we should therefore expect a form **Terga-finnas*, not *Ter-finnas*, in Alfred's text. It may perhaps be suggested that a compound **Teria-finnar* was altered to **Ter-finnar*[15] in OWN. (hence OE. *Ter-finnas*) on

á) and Finn. *u*, cf. Lapp. *mânne* : Finn. *muna* 'egg,' Lapp. *bâdnet* 'to spin' : Finn. *punoa* 'to twist, plait.'   [14] So Vasmer IV, 177.
[15] According to S. Egilsson and F. Jónsson, *Lexicon poeticum antiquæ linguæ septentrionalis* s.v. *Tyrfifinnar*, the name of the *Terfinnas* actually does appear in Norse, in one of the stanzas from Qrvar-Odds Saga, in the Ævidrápa (st. 9) *viz.*

the analogy of compounds such as OIcel. *bryn-glófi, brynhattr, bryn-hosa, bryn-stúka* besides *brynia* and *smið-belgr* besides *smiðia*.[16] In concluding this section it may be noted that *Trinnes, Trennes*,[17] the mediaeval Scandinavian name, first for Ponoi (at the mouth of the river of that name) together with the adjacent promontory Cape Korabel'nyi (the most easterly point of the Kola Peninsula),[18] but, later for the eastern part and even the whole of the peninsula,[19] cannot be considered to derive from an earlier Norse form in **Ter-* (with metathesis)[20] and thus be brought into connection with Alfred's *Ter-*; it merely contains the ORuss. *Trě, Tьrě* discussed above.[21]

(Jónsson B. II. 326 and A. II. 307):—" My two wise kinsmen were the leaders on the warships; the wise rowers wished to possess the property which the *Tyrfifinnar* had." The MS. has *tyfvi finnar* and Jónsson wishes to take this as an error for **Tyrfi-finnar*, the first element being a corruption of **Ter-* by reason of folk-etymology (he was presumably thinking of a folk-etymology with the name of the well-known sword *Tyrfingr*). Jónsson's suggestion seems probable and it is perhaps significant that, here also, the *Terfinnas* are in juxtaposition to the *Beormas*— the *Bjarmar* are mentioned in the stanzas immediately preceding and following the one quoted. It seems however probable that in this case the form underlying the folk-etymology is not **Ter-* or **Teria* < PrLapp. **Tārjā* but rather an OWN. **Tyria* < PrBF. **Turja* (= Finn. *Turja*—see above). And the reading **Tyrvi-finnar* may be suggested as more probable than Jónsson's **Tyrfi-finnar*; this would be closer to the manuscript and the folk-etymology would in this case be with OIcel. *tyrue* ' fir-wood containing tarry substances '—doubtless an allusion to the habit of smearing the face with a preparation of wood-tar as a prophylactic against mosquitoes which is well-known among the Lapps (cf. G. von Düben, *Om Lappland och lapparne* p. 85) as elsewhere in North Europe and Asia (see *Tietosanakirja* s.v. *Pikiöljy*).
[16] The much discussed subject of the chronology of *i*-umlaut in Old West Norse is naturally relevant to the whole of the question discussed above. It will suffice to say that the late ninth-century phonology which is postulated here does not conflict with any of the different views on the point (for literature see BN §78 note 1). [17] For references see Johnsen, *Register* s.v. *Trinnes*. [18] Johnsen p. 26. [19] Johnsen p. 80, note 165. [20] Cf. Icel. *freta* = OHG. *fërzan*.
[21] The form *crefenne* occurs as a variant reading for the accepted (*gentes*) *Scrierefennae* (*Screre-* is a corruption of **Screde-* i.e. **Scridi-* —cf. OE. *Scride-finnas*) in Jordanes' *Getica* (ed. Th. Mommsen) iii. 21. A. C. Lehrberg, *Untersuchungen zur Erläuterung der älteren Geschichte Russlands* (1816) p. 205 note 3, (tacitly) emends *cre-* to **tre-* (the emendation would actually have to be to **ter-* —cf. p. 25) and takes the word as the *Terfinnas*. Vasmer IV, 177 note 6 rightly rejects this very improbable suggestion on the grounds that Jordanes could hardly have been cognisant of the Kola Peninsula.

THE *BEORMAS*

I. EVIDENCE.

The identity of Ohthere's *Beormas* with the people called *Bjarmar* in Old West Norse is so obvious that it has never been questioned.[1] I now proceed to give the Scandinavian[2] evidence relating to Bjarmaland and the Bjarmar, arranged under three heads:—(A) Icelandic, (B) Scandinavian Latin, (C) Cartography.

(A) Icelandic[3]

(i) *Heimskringla* (ed. F. Jónsson, 1911).

(1) " After that he [sc. Eiríkr] went north to Finmark and right to Bjarmaland and there he had a great battle and was victorious " (p. 61, line 26 ff.).

(2) " One summer Haraldr Gráfeldr went with his army north to Bjarmaland, and harried there and had a great battle with the Bjarmar on the bank of the Dvina. King Haraldr was victorious and slew many people; then he harried the country far and wide and got a vast amount of money. Glúmr Geirason says of this:—' The subjugator of kings, bold in words, reddened the sword in the East, north of the burning settlement, where I saw the Bjarmian people run; the setter of treaties among men obtained fame on that expedition; the young prince had a battle on the Dvina's bank.' " (p. 102, line 4 ff.; Jónsson B. I. 66-7).

[1] From the philological point of view Alfred's *Beormas* represents OWN. *Bjarmar* exactly; see *Acta Philologica Scandinavica* [June 1940: reference not available] and LSE. vi, 5.
[2] Some of the Icelandic sources are collected in C. C. Rafn, *Antiquités russes* (1850-52); cf. also Smirnov, *Permjaki* and S. K. Kuznetsov, *K voprosu o Biarmij* [On the question of Biarmia] (*Etnograficheskoe obozrenie* 55-56).
[3] I confine myself to Icelandic references in which Bjarmaland or the Bjarmar are specifically mentioned. There are further a number of episodes in the sagas which probably refer to Bjarmaland although the name is not actually mentioned. Mrs. N. K. Chadwick is dealing with these—also with *Glæsisvellir* (see pp. 43-4)—in a forthcoming work. I refrain from discussing the difficult question of possible references to Bjarmaland in the folk-literature of Scandinavia—Icelandic *rímur* (except certain references, see below), Færoese ballads and the *folkeviser*.

(3) " King Hákon . . . had been north to Bjarmaland; he had a battle there and was victorious " (p. 519, line 29 ff.). (4) Karli hinn háleyski, his brother Gunnsteinn and Þórir hundr go on a trading-venture to Bjarmaland. " And when they came to Bjarmaland they put in at a trading-station; then trading began; all the men with them who had money to spend got plenty of goods. Þórir got a quantity of furs: grey squirrel, beaver and sable. Karli also had very much money with which he bought many skins. And when the market was finished they held down the Dvina; it was then an end to peace with the natives." When they are out to sea a meeting is held and Þórir arranges an expedition, which promises danger but much booty: he said that in Bjarmaland " when rich men died their chattels had to be divided between the dead man and his heirs; the dead man had to have a half or a third (but sometimes less); the property had to be carried out into the forest—sometimes to mounds—and buried; sometimes a building was put over it." They go ashore; "first of all there were level plains and then a great forest . . . . They came out into a large clearing and, in the clearing, there was a high palisade (skíðgarðr) with a door which was locked in front. Six of the natives were supposed to guard the palisade each night, two for each third of the night." But they find it unguarded and effect an entry. " Þórir said ' In this enclosure there is a mound in which gold and silver and earth are all mixed together; that is your objective. But in the enclosure there stands the god of the Bjarmar who is called Jomali; let no one be so bold as to plunder him.' Then they went to the mound and took as many things as possible; they carried them in their clothes; much earth was mixed therewith as was to be expected." Þórir now tells the party to leave but he " returned to Jomali and took a silver bowl which was standing on his knees; it was full of silver coins; he poured the silver into his kirtle and put the chain of the bowl over his arm; then he went out to the doorway. By this time

all the others were out of the palisade; now they noticed that Þórir had stayed behind. Karli went back to look for him and they met inside the doorway; Karli saw that Þórir had the silver bowl with him. Then Karli ran to the jomali; he saw that there was a thick necklet on his neck. Karli swung his axe at it and severed the strap at the back of the neck by which the necklet was held. The blow was so great that Jomali's head flew off; the crash was such that everybody was amazed. Karli took the necklet and then they went away. And as soon as the crash came the watchmen came out into the clearing and immediately blew their horns; then they heard the sound of trumpets on all sides of them." The Bjarmar pursue them but they reach the ships in safety and depart. (p. 311 ff.).

(ii) *Egilssaga Skallagrímssonar* (ed. S. Nordal, 1933):—
" And one spring Eiríkr blóðøx made ready an expedition to Bjarmaland . . . Of this expedition there was much to relate: Eiríkr had a great battle in Bjarmaland on the Dvina; Eiríkr gained a victory there, as it says in the verses about him." (p. 93).

(iii) *Fagrskinna* (ed. F. Jónsson, 1902-03):—" . . . he [sc. Eiríkr] went plundering north to Finmark and as far as Bjarmaland." (p. 30, line 17 ff.).

(iv) *Kormakssaga* (ed. Th. Möbius, 1886):—" Then, in the spring, King Haraldr prepared an expedition to Bjarmaland, with a great number of men. Kormakr was captain of one ship on that expedition, Þorvaldr of another; there are no other captains named . . . After that they went to Bjarmaland and came back." (Chap. 25).

(v) *Landnámabók*.

(1) " King Hjǫrr harried in Bjarmaland. As part of the booty he took captive Ljúfvina, daughter of the King of the Bjarmar." (*Hauksbók* and *Sturlubók*, ed. of F. Jónsson (1900): p. 38, line 7 ff. and p. 161, line 27 ff.).

(2) " Þorgeirr hǫggvinkinni was a retainer of King Hákon Aðalsteinsfóstri. And when he was prepared to go to

Bjarmaland, Haraldr came with a great army. Then
Þorgeirr recited the following:—[here follows a verse of
Eyvindr Finnsson's (Jónsson B. I. 62, Lausavísur 2); it has
no bearing on Bjarmaland]." (Later *Melabók*, ed. of F.
Jónsson (1921): p. 35, line 7 ff.).
(vi) *Flateyjarbók* (ed. of 1860-68).

(1) One summer King Haraldr sends Haukr and Víghardr
north to Bjarmaland and to the dwelling of Heiðr on the
White Sea,[4] to fetch furs. King Eiríkr hears of the expedition
and tells Bjǫrn and Salgarðr to go north to Bjarmaland.
Haukr and Víghardr fight a battle with the latter in the
White Sea. All the protagonists are killed save Haukr who
returns to Heiðr. She takes him to "where the merchants
are"; he leaves her and returns to King Haraldr (i, 579 ff.).

(2) On the death of Valdamarr his three sons divide his
kingdom. Búrizláfr has Kiev (*Kænugarðr*), Jarizleifr
Novgorod (*Holmgarðr*) and Vartiláfr the domains of Polotsk
(*Palteskja*). Eymundr and his men come to Jarizleifr at
Novgorod. Búrizláfr demands from Jarizleifr certain parts
of the latter's kingdom. Jarizleifr refuses this demand
whereupon Búrizláfr attacks him, but is defeated and flees to
Bjarmaland; Búrizláfr makes another attack on Jarizleifr
with an army of Bjarmar but is again defeated and put to
flight. This time he flees to the land of the Turks and once
more attacks Jarizleifr. Búrizláfr is killed. Eymundr now
goes to Vartiláfr; Jarizleifr in turn demands some of
Vartiláf's territory but, with the aid of Eymundr, a com-
promise is ultimately reached: Jarizleifr keeps Novgorod,
Vartiláfr takes Kiev and Eymundr Polotsk (*Eymundar
þáttr* ii, 118 ff.).[5]

[4] I translate *Gandvík* by ' White Sea ' throughout, though I postpone the detailed
discussion of the name (and in particular of its relation to Finn. *Kannan-lahti*
' Kandalaks Bay ') to a later article.
[5] The events dealt with here took place after the death of St. Vladimir in 1015;
the Norse Búrizláfr, Jarizleifr and Vartiláfr correspond, respectively, to the Russian
Svjatopolk, Jaroslav and Brjacheslav. In the Russian version there is no mention
of Bjarmaland (i.e. *Zavoloche*—see pp. 56-7); Svjatopolk's first place of refuge is
given as Poland and, in one source, as the country of the Pechenegs. The detailed

(3) "*The expedition of Andrés and Ívarr.* This summer Andrés skjaldarband and Ívarr útvík made an expedition to Bjarmaland. They had four ships. And the reason for the expedition was as follows. A few years previously Andrés of Sannmælingar, Sveinn Sigurðarson, Ǫgmundr of Spangheimr and many others had had a trading-venture to Bjarmaland. They had two ships and Andrés and Sveinn came back in the autumn, but Helgi Bógrangsson and his crew remained behind with the second ship. Ǫgmundr of Spangheimr also remained behind; and in the autumn he went east[6] to Suzdal'[7] with his men and wares. And hostilities broke out between the men of Helgeland and the King of the Bjarmar and, in the winter, the Bjarmar attacked them and killed all the ship's crew. And when Ǫgmundr heard this he came from the east to Novgorod, then east and down to the sea; and he did not stop until he came to Jerusalem; thence he went up to Norway; this expedition of his was very famous.[8] Andrés and Ívarr went to Bjarmaland and ravaged there very much; they slaughtered and plundered and got very great wealth in furs and refined silver . . . In the autumn Andrés went to Helgeland and since then there have been no journeys to Bjarmaland." (iii, 49 ff.).[9]

(4) " Many Bjarmar who had fled from the East, from the hostility of the *Tattarar*[10] came to him [*sc.* King Hákon];

discussion of the considerable discrepancy between the Russian and Scandinavian versions does not therefore concern us here; it will suffice to refer to A. I. Ljashchenko, " Eymundar Saga " i russkie letopisi [The " Eymundar Saga " and the Russian Chronicles], *Izvestija Akademii Nauk* 1926 pp. 1061-86.

[6] Actually much more south than east.

[7] *Sydridala riki.* Tiander p. 434 takes this as Suzdal'; this is probably correct—the form may well be due to a folk-etymology. Suzdal' is mentioned in a more correct form elsewhere in Scandinavian sources cf., for instance, *Surdalar*, Heimslýsing ok helgifrœði (*Hauksbók*, ed. of 1892-96, p. 155 line 19); *af Surdolum* Flat. iii, 187; and—in juxtaposition to Bjarmaland—*til Surtzdala* in Flat. 1 above (i, 579).

[8] Deservedly so, if authentic—but I must leave to the specialist the discussion of its historicity.

[9] There is also a notice of this expedition in the Annals *s.a.* 1222 : in the Flateyjarbók annals (iii, 526), in the Annales Reseniani, in the annals of Henrik Høyer, in the Annales Regii, in the Skálholt annals and in the annals of Gottskalk (see G. Storm, *Islandske Annaler indtil* 1578).

[10] See pp. 46-8.

he baptised them and gave them the fjord which is called Malangen." (iii, 232). (vii) *Bósasaga*[11] (ed. O. L. Jiriczek, 1893). Bósi and Herrauðr are sent to Bjarmaland to bring back a fabulous vulture's egg. " They held to the east, came to Bjarmaland and made fast alongside a stretch of virgin forest (*eyðiskógr*).[12] The king who ruled there at that time was called Hárekr " (p. 21). They go on a reconnaissance and meet a man called Hóketill who, with the aid of his daughter, entertains them well. In the night the daughter says to Bósi: " Here in this forest there stands a great temple; it belongs to King Hárekr . . . there is a mighty god there, who is called Jomali (*v.r.* Jomanni); there is much gold and treasure there " (p. 25). She further tells him that King Hárek's mother, Kolfrosta, who is a witch and in charge of the temple, has abducted Hleiðr, the sister of the neighbouring king, Guðmundr of Glæsisvellir, with the intent that Hleiðr shall succeed to the office of temple-priestess. In the temple there is—apart from the vulture and its egg—a slave who " looks after the priestess' food; she needs a two-year old heifer at every meal . . . There is a bull in the temple, bewitched and enchanted; he is bound with iron bands; he has to cover the heifer; then she becomes impregnated with poison and everyone who eats is bewitched; they will prepare such a heifer for Hleiðr, the King's sister, and she will then become a troll, like the priestess " (p. 26). Bósi and Herrauðr go to the temple and, slaying the slave, the priestess and the vulture, they find much gold and also the egg. " They went to the altar where Jomali (*v.r.* Jomanus) was sitting; they took from him a gold crown set with 12 gems and a collar that would have cost 300 gold marks; and from his knees they took a silver bowl so large that four men could not have emptied it; it was full

---

[11] There are three versions:—(1) the earlier Bósasaga (2) the Bósarímur and (3) the later Bósasaga. The Bósarímur were apparently composed about the year 1500; they are based on the earlier Bósasaga but are embellished. The later Bósasaga probably reflects the prototype of the earlier version; it is however embellished and also influenced by the Bósarímur.
[12] Later called *Vínuskógr*.

of red gold; and the cloth that was spread over Jomali (*v.r.* the jomali) was worth more than three cargoes from the richest dromond that sails the Grecian sea; all this they took for themselves " (p. 29 ff.). In a carefully-hidden recess they find Hleiðr; they take her with them, burn the temple and depart. The rest of the story is complicated and, as it does not add anything to our knowledge of the Bjarmar, may safely be omitted here.[13]

(viii) *Hálfssaga ok Hálfsrekka* (ed. A. Le Roy Andrews, 1909.) Hjǫrleifr takes an expedition to Bjarmaland, to the mouth of the Dvina; they break open a mound and gain much booty (chap. 5).

(ix) *Hálfdanarsaga Brǫnufóstra* (ed. in Rafn). The children Hálfdan and Ingibjǫrg are sent to Óttarr of Bjarmaland. When Hálfdan is twelve Óttarr gives him four ships and he voyages widely during the summer but, when he tries to return to Bjarmaland in the autumn, he finds himself in Labrador (*Helluland*) instead.

(x) *Hálfdanarsaga Eysteinssonar.* The plot of this saga is very involved and to summarise it would require a disproportionate amount of space. It will suffice to refer the reader to the excellent edition of F. R. Schröder (1917) and to say that, in our context, the point of interest is the mention of various campaigns between Bjarmaland and the country round Lake Ladoga of which the chief town was *Aldeigjuborg* i.e. Staraja Ladoga.[14]

(xi) *Sturlaugssaga Starfsama* (ed. in Rafn). Sturlaugr is sent in search of a magic urochs-horn. In Hundingjaland he is told " that there is a temple standing in Bjarmaland; it is

[13] Substantially the same story is found in the later Bósasaga. Interesting points are:—(1) On the expedition to Bjarmaland they find a dwelling in the forest (here called *Myrkviskógur* ' wood of darkness '—cf. *myrkviðr* of the same meaning, applied to various forests both real and mythical) and ask their whereabouts; they are told that the country is ' Eastern Bjarmaland ' (*Bjarmaland austara*); (2) the priestess is served by " twelve other witch-women "; (3) the temple lies in the wood, to the east of their starting-point.

[14] For this identification see J. J. Mikkola, " Ladoga, Laatokka," SUSA XXIII. xxiii (with references to further literature).

dedicated to Þórr and Óðinn, Frigg and Freyja and cunningly wrought of the most precious wood; there are two doors into the temple, one from the north-west and one from the south-west; inside Þórr is alone and, before him on a table, is the urochs-horn" (Chap. 17). Sturlaugr is advised to enter the temple alone and not to touch the horn with bare hands for "it is full of poison and magic" (*ibid.*). After various adventures they leave Hundingjaland and " they sail till they reach Bjarmaland and are in front of the Dvina. To the west of the river they see level plains; there was there a temple so resplendent that it seemed to illumine all the plains for it was adorned with gold and precious stones" (Chap. 18). They go ashore: "they go to the door which was on the northwest of the temple, for this was the only one that was open; then they saw that over the threshold there was a pit full of poison, and just beyond it a great bar, fixed over the entrance; and there was brick-work in the doorway round the pit so that the fittings should not be spoilt by an excess of poison" (*ibid.*). Sturlaugr " looks into the temple and sees Þórr, very tall, sitting in the high-seat; in front of him was a fine table coated with silver; he sees that the urochshorn is standing in front of Þórr on the table; it was as beautiful as gold to look on, and it was full of poison. He saw a backgammon-board and men (*taflborð ok tafl*) standing there, both made of shining gold; resplendent garments and golden rings were fastened up on poles. There were sixty women in the temple and there was one who surpassed them all; she was as big as a giant . . . she served before the table" (*ibid.*). Sturlaugr seizes the horn and escapes from the giant templepriestess and from the Bjarmar who have heard the uproar in the temple; they sail away. Later we are told of another expedition of Sturlaug's to Bjarmaland; he ravages the land, defeats the Bjarmar under Rǫndólfr their king (whom he slays) and subjugates the country. Towards the end of the story Sturlaugr ascertains the origin of the magic urochs-horn from Mjǫll, the King of Finmark's daughter.

She tells him that, owing to the ravages of King Haraldr, there was a widespread famine which was particularly bad in Bjarmaland; "then they took a certain animal and worshipped it; they called it ' urochs ' (*úrr*) . . . then it began to eat both men and cattle and it subjugated everybody, laying waste everything west of the River Dvina, so that nothing living escaped " (Chap. 22). King Haraldr heard of this, went to Bjarmaland and, with the aid of a woman called Guðríðr, killed the urochs; she took its single horn as her reward.

(xii) *Qrvar-Oddssaga* (ed. R. C. Boer, 1888). *S*-version: Oddr and his men " came to Bjarmaland and put their ships up into the River Dvina.[15] And when they had come there the natives immediately heard news of it; men were sent to meet them and a fortnight's truce was appointed for a market; the natives came down with all kinds of furs; of these all those who had anything to exchange got a quantity. This time elapsed and there was an end to the truce; Oddr and his men then rode at anchor out in the river." That evening Oddr suggests that he and Ásmundr should make a reconnaissance ashore. " When they had landed they went into the forest. In the forest they saw a great hall; by now it was very dark. They went up to the door; they saw that it was light inside so that there was no shadow anywhere; there was a large company inside and revelry and drinking. Then Oddr said ' Do you understand anything of the language of the people here ? ' Ásmundr says ' No more than the twittering of birds; do you understand anything ? ' Oddr said ' You can see that there is a man serving both the benches and I suspect that he may be able to talk Norwegian. Now you are to wait for me while I go inside.' Ásmundr does so.

---

[15] The *M*-version adds: " there are many islands lying in the river. They cast anchor there under the spit which comes down from the mainland and into the river." Apart from this the differences between the two versions are not of any particular interest in the present context. Further on the later version *A* interpolates a long and rather fantastic story about Bjarmaland which lack of space prevents me summarising (p. 126 ff.).

Oddr now enters and stands by the dresser which was near the door, where there was at least the chance that a shadow would be cast." Oddr boldly carries off the cup-bearer and returns to the ship with him. Under compulsion the cup-bearer submits to questioning; he tells Oddr that he has been there seven years and that he is a Norwegian by birth; as to possible plunder he says: " There is a mound standing higher up the River Dvina, composed of earth and bright coins; they have to carry there a double handful of silver and a double handful of earth for each man who dies and also for those who are born." Oddr remains in charge of the ships and the cup-bearer, and an expedition is sent to the mound; it returns with much plunder. Oddr now leads an expedition to the mound himself. They are returning back along the river, loaded, when he espies a great host of Bjarmar coming out of the forest (these have been warned by the cup-bearer who has managed to escape from the ship). "Oddr said: ' You must make towards the river and take up your position across that projection which juts out into it.'" After a parley with the Bjarmar (represented by the cup-bearer) in which Oddr refuses to sell arms to them and after he has warned his men " if any of our troop fall, be sure to take any who are dead and throw them out into the river—for, if they get hold of a dead man, they will at once cast spells on our troop," a fierce battle[16] ensues in which they defeat the Bjarmar. They rejoin their comrades and sail away—to Finmark—with much plunder. (p. 27 ff.).[17]

[16] In a stanza occurring later in the saga reference to *two* battles with the Bjarmar is made:—" You, Sigurðr, lay in the maidens' hall, whilst I fought twice against the Bjarmar; swiftly as hawks we fought a battle while you, man, slept under the coverlet in the hall " (Jónsson B. II. 318, St. 8).

[17] Of minor references in the sagas I may mention:—*Brennu-Njálssaga* (ed. F. Jónsson, 1908) " He said that he had sailed between all the countries which were between Norway and Russia—' and I have also sailed to Bjarmaland ' " (p. 64, line 8 ff.); *Heiðrekssaga* (ed. Jón Helgason, 1924) " Arngrímr was at that time on a viking expedition in the East, round Bjarmaland " (p. 3, line 30 ff.); *Ánssaga Bogsveigis* (ed. in Rafn), *B*-version " [Þórir] harried Bjarmaland after this, and got great booty " (ii, 360 note 1); on the Huldarsaga see p. 63. It may be noted finally that the runic manuscript of the Historia Hialmari Regis

(xiii) *Landafræði* (ed. in K. Kålund, *Alfræði Íslenzk* vol. I).

(1) " Next to Denmark there is Sweden the less; then there is Öland; then there is Gotland; then Hälsingland; then Värmland; then the 2 Cwen-lands—and these are north of Bjarmaland. From Bjarmaland uninhabited territories run north until Greenland starts." (p. 12, line 5 ff.).

(2) " Finmark is north of Norway. Thence the land trends north-east and then again east before one reaches Bjarmaland which is tributary to the King of Russia." (p. 11, line 11 ff.: *v.r.*).[17a]

(B) Scandinavian Latin

(i) *Saxonis Gesta Danorum* (ed. J. Olrik and H. Ræder, 1931).

(1) Thuningus (*v.r.* Turingus) collects a band of Byarmenses (*v.r.* Warmenses) and joins battle with Hadingus . . . " Tunc Byarmenses arma artibus permutantes carminibus in nimbos solvere cælum lætamque aeris faciem tristi imbrium aspergine confuderunt." (I. viii. §16).

(2) " Ea tempestate Helgo Halogiæ rex Gusonis (*MS.* Cusonis) Finnorum Byarmorumque principis filiam nomine Thoram crebræ legationis officio procabatur." (III. ii. §8).

(3) " Quem (*sc.* Arngrimum pugilem Sueticum) Ericus hortari cœpit, ut . . . pugnaretque adversum Egtherum regem Biarmiæ et Thengillum regem Finnimarchiæ, quod ii soli, ceteris obsequentibus, Danicum detrectare viderentur imperium . . . Deinde Egtherum Biarmiæ ducem duello provocatum devicit indiditque condicionem Biarmis viritim pellem pro capite persolvendi." (V. xiii. §§1-2).[18]

Biarmlandiæ atque Thulemarkiæ (see G. Hickes, *Linguarum Vett. Septentrionalium Thesaurus Grammatico-criticus et archæologicus: Dissertatio Epistolaris* p. 123 ff.) published as *Fragmentvm Mscr. Runici* . . . *sub Præsidio Joannis Bilberg* at Upsala in 1690 is (*teste* Professor O. von Friesen) accepted as a forgery of the late seventeenth century.

[17a] In conclusion it may be noted that *bjarmalandsför* (also *bjarmalandsferð* ?) is to some extent in use in Modern Icelandic in the sense ' wild-goose-chase ', though this sense is not recorded by the dictionaries. Professor Bruce Dickins calls my attention to J. Thoroddsen, *Maður og Kona*, Ch. XIX title, *Bjarmalandsför Egils*.

[18] Cf. also Thomas Gheysmerus (Langebek ii, 315) and Petrus Olavi (Langebek i, 89).

(4) "... Starcatherus ab athletis Biarmensibus ob virtutem accitus, cum plurima apud eos memoratu digna edidisset facinora, Sueonum fines ingreditur." (VI. v. §10). Cf. also "Ad hæc Starcatherus ... 'pugilesque subegi Biarmenses (v.r. peremi Biermenses)'." (VIII. viii. §9).[19]

(5) Gormo and Thorkillus are making an expedition to the dwelling of Geruthus. Leaving Helgeland "optato vento excepti in ulteriorem Byarmiam navigant. Regio est perpetui frigoris capax præaltisque offusa nivibus, ne vim quidem fervoris persentiscit æstivi, inviorum abundans nemorum, frugum haud ferax inusitatisque alibi bestiis frequens. Crebri in ea fluvii ob insitas alveis cautes stridulo spumantique volumine perferuntur." In Byarmia they are met by Guthmundus who leads them further to the dwelling of his brother Geruthus, whence, after many miraculous adventures, they ultimately return home. (VIII. xiv).

(6) "At Regnerus ... Biarmos nuper devictos invalida subiectionis fide palam imperium detrectantes invenit. Qui cum adventum eius compertum haberent, carminibus aggressi cælum, sollicitatas nubes ad summam usque nimborum violentiam impulerunt. Quæ res Danos aliquamdiu navigatione prohibitos alimentorum facultate defecit. Eosdem quoque, subito remissa tempestate, æstuosissimi fervoris flagrantia torruit. Nec ea quidem pestis concitati frigoris magnitudine tolerabilior exstitit ... Ceterum laxi ventris profluvium complurimos exanimavit. Ita Danorum plerique, dubia cæli qualitate conclusi, passim, oborta corporum pestilentia, decesserunt." Regnerus sails away—to Kurland—but returns to Byarmia and makes a sudden attack. The Bjarmian king (whose name is not known) "Matullum Finmarchiæ ducem perfugio petiit. Cuius peritissima sagittariorum opera fretus Regneri apud Biarmiam hiberna peragentem impune laceravit exercitum." But ultimately Regnerus was victorious and "Ubi Biarmorum

---

[19] The passage in Thomas Gheysmerus (Langebek ii, 318) is directly due to Saxo; so also, but less directly, is the *Starkaðarsaga Stórvirkssonar* (ed. Winnipeg, 1911).

rege interfecto, Finnorum vero fugato, Regnerus saxis rerum gestarum apices præ se ferentibus iisdemque superne locatis æternum victoriæ suæ monumentum affixit." (IX. iv. §§22-25).[20]

(ii) *Historia Norwegiæ* (ed. in G. Storm, *Monumenta Historica Norvegiæ*).

(1) "Versus vero septemtrionem gentes perplures paganismo (proh dolor) inservientes trans Norwegiam ab oriente extenduntur, scilicet Kiriali et Kwæni, cornuti Finni ac utrique Biarmones. Sed quæ gentes post istos habitent, nihil certum habemus. Quidam tamen nautæ cum de Glaciali insula ad Norwegiam remeare studuissent et a contrariis ventorum turbinibus in brumalem plagam propulsi essent, inter Viridenses et Biarmones tandem applicuerunt, ubi homines miræ magnitudinis et virginum terram (quæ gustu aquæ concipere dicuntur) se reperisse protestati sunt." (p. 74, line 3 ff.).

(2) "Quarta Halogia . . . quæ patria in aquilonem terminat Norwegiam juxta locum Wegestaf,[21] qui Biarmoniam ab ea dirimit. Ibi ille profundissimus septentrionalis sinus, qui Charybdim, Scyllam et inevitabiles voragines in se continet . . . ." (p. 78, line 1 ff.).[22]

[20] Cf. also Thomas Gheysmerus (Langebek ii, 342-3) and Petrus Olavi (Langebek i, 110).

[21] This may safely be taken as Svjatoi Nos; see Storm, *op. cit.* p. 78 note 3; Johnsen p. 17 ff.

[22] The accounts of Biarmia in Olaus Magnus' *Historia de gentibus septentrionalibus* (Rome, 1555) pp. 9-10 and in his brother Johannes Magnus' *Historia de omnibus Gothorum Sveonumque Regibus* (Rome, 1554) p. 8 are, in the main, due to Saxo (see K. Ahlenius, *Olaus Magnus och hans framställning af nordens geografi* p. 120). Olaus' statement (p. 10) "Diuiditur autem Biarmia, secundum Saxonem Sialandicum, in vlteriorem, & citeriorem " is of particular interest (cf. p. 43). In the instructions issued to the Dano-Norwegian emissaries for the meeting suggested by Christian IV to determine the frontier with Russia in Kola, held 1st July 1595 (see Johnsen pp. 312-14), it is stated that " vonn alters der ambtman vonn Wardthusen [i.e. Vardø] seine dienere über mehr geschigkt unnd auch in Bermelandt den schatz samblen und holen laβen." This would appear merely to be a vague reference to the Bjarmaland Voyages of the sagas (see further Johnsen p. 99 ff.). *Biarmia* is also mentioned in a letter of Ivan IV to Karl V of 1556 which is preserved in Danmarks Rigsarkiv, Copenhagen (Johnsen p. 100, note 241). To list all the references to Biarmia in the sixteenth and later centuries would be an impossible and unprofitable task. I may however mention here the remarks in

(C) Cartography

As would be expected the Bjarmar are indicated on the Old Icelandic planisphere: *Biarmar habitauit* (sic) *hic* appears as the sole entry in the NNW. semi-octant.[23] An entry *Biarmia* is not found on Claudius Claussøn's map,[24] nor—naturally—on the portolani; it is also absent from Jakob Ziegler's map of Norway, Sweden, Finland etc. (1531).[25] In Olaus Magnus' *Carta Marina* (1539),[26] *Biarmia* is entered on the land north of the 'Lacus Albus,' clearly corresponding to the Kola Peninsula. The entry of *Biarmia* in this position is of interest (cf. p. 43); it is certainly due to Olaus Magnus' interpretation of Saxo's information about Biarmia (cf. Ahlenius, *op. cit.* p. 124) but tradition may also have played a part. The entry of *Biarmia* on the Kola Peninsula is naturally also found in those maps which derive from the *Carta Marina*. A list of these is given by Ahlenius, *op. cit.* p. 427 ff. so there is no necessity to enumerate them here.[27]

II. IDENTIFICATION.

We may now proceed to a discussion of the information contained in the above quotations. But in this connection the attitude of the Scandinavians to the subject should be borne in mind : to them Bjarmaland was on the very confines of the world and, although they have preserved for us much information that is valuable, most of it—Ohthere's narrative

---

J. Matalius' 'Præfatio et Commentarius' to H. Osorius, *De rebus Emmanuelis, Lusitaniae Regis* (Cologne ed. of 1581, pp. 26v.-27r.) and in the letter of Guðbrandur Þorláksson, Bishop of Hólar, printed by Hakluyt (*The Principal Navigations Voyages Traffiques & Discoveries of the English Nation*, ed. of 1914; iv, 194 ff.).
[23] K. Kalund, *Alfræði Íslenzk* iii, Plate to face p. 120.
[24] See A. Bjørnbo and C. S. Petersen, *Der Däne Claudius Claussøn Swart*.
[25] J. Ziegler, *Quae intus continentur. Syria . . . . . Schondia . . . . .* (1532): Octava Tabula.
[26] Facs. ed. of 1887.
[27] I may however add here that *Biarmia* is also found entered due south of Vardø in J. and B. van Doetichum, *Tabula hydrographica, tum maris Baltici . . . tum Septentrionalis Oceani navigationem continens* (Amsterdam, 1589) and in the map of Joris Carolus of 1614 which is reproduced in F. C. Wieder, *The Dutch discovery and mapping of Spitsbergen* (1596-1829), Plate 5.

is a notable exception—is coloured by a romantic attitude and intermingled with fictions imported from diverse sources. After eliminating such elements as magic (cf. e.g. Bósas., Sts.st., Saxo 1 and 6) and giants (cf. e.g. Hist.N. 1) we may classify the information remaining under the following heads:—

(i) *Situation.* We have the very strongest evidence that the River Dvina (: OIcel. *Vina*)[1] was in Bjarmian territory; cf. Hkr. 2 and 4, Eg.s., Bósas., Hálfss., Sts.st., Qr.Os. On the other hand Ohthere's *Beormas* were, as we have seen, not on the Dvina but on Kandalaks Bay, near the Terfinnas, on the west side of the White Sea. The " utrique Biarmones " of Hist.N 1, the " ulterior Byarmia " of Saxo 5 and the " Eastern Bjarmaland " of Bósas.[2] thus become clear : Bjarmaland was divided into two parts, *Biarmia ulterior* in which the Dvina was situated and *Biarmia citerior* in which Ohthere's *Beormas* on Kandalaks Bay were situated; the entry *Biarmia* on Olaus Magnus' *Carta Marina* would appear to refer to the latter.[2]

To the country east of East Bjarmaland we have but the scantiest references; as Hist. N. 1 expresses it " quæ gentes post istos [sc. Biarmones] habitent, nihil certum habemus'. Bjarmaland was really the end of the world (cf. Hist. N. 2). Ld.fr.1 tells us that it is joined by a strip of uninhabited territory to Greenland and in Hfds.Br. it is evidently envisaged as adjacent to America. Ohthere was a cautious man and did not relate the " many tales " which the Beormas told him. The *Glæsisvellir* of Bósas. clearly lies to the east of East Bjarmaland, but, although it is ruled by a king with a Norse name, *Guðmundr* (and cf. also Saxo 5), we should certainly hesitate in accepting it as a real Norse sphere of influence still further east; everything we hear

---

[1] On the name see a forthcoming article by A. S. C. Ross.

[2] We should not of course be justified in concluding from the " utrique Biarmones " of Hist. N. 1 that the inhabitants of the two parts of Bjarmaland were racially distinct, for this expression may only mean the ' inhabitants of the two Biarmiae.'

about it points to it existing purely in the realms of fiction and to this view its obviously mythological name (: Icel. *glæsiligr* ' shining, splendid ') lends support.

(ii) *Natural History.* Only in Saxo 5³ do we find any attempt at an actual description of the country; the other references are incidental. The point that seems to have struck all travellers is the huge forests—the *Vínuskógr* of Bósas.; cf. also Hkr. 4 and Qr.Os. Between the sea and the forest there were, according to Hkr. 4 (and cf. also Sts.st.), "level plains" i.e. tundras. In Qr.Os. we hear of a *nes* projecting into the River Dvina, somewhere near its mouth; this will have been an alluvial projection, similar to those found in the river to-day; and in the M-version of this saga there is a reference to islands in the Dvina and a projection at its mouth; conditions were doubtless similar to those obtaining to-day, though of course the modern topography is of quite recent alluvial formation.[4]

The descriptive details as to the natural history given above are reasonably accurate and require no further comment. There is however one point which presents difficulties; this is the interpretation of Ohthere's antithesis between the *gebun land* of the Beormas and the *weste land* of the Terfinnas. There are, at first sight, two possibilities: the antithesis may be 1) between inhabited and uninhabited land or 2) between cultivated and uncultivated land.

The semantics of the words *gebūn* (and the closely-related adj. *bȳne*)[5] and *wēste* afford no help for either meaning is possible for either word : OE. *wēste* can mean either uninhabited or uncultivated or, naturally, both together; OE. *(ge)būan* trans. normally means 'to occupy' and it is admittedly not recorded in a passage which renders the sense ' to cultivate ' unambiguous; but the latter sense is plentifully

[3] See also p. 61.
[4] See the 1:1,500,000 *Carte géologique internationale de l'Europe* (1881-1913), Sheet 12.
[5] The morphology of Goth. *báuan* (3rd weak) OIcel. *búa* (strong, reduplicating) is difficult; but OE. *bȳne* adj. would appear to stand in much the same relation to OE. *ge-būn* p. part. as WS. *ge-sīene* adj. does to WS. *ge-sewen* p. part. of *sēon*.

attested in all the other branches of West Germanic—MHG. *búwen*[6] MnHG. *bauen* (cf. particularly *das land bauen* ' agrum colere ')[7] MLG. *buwen*[8] MDu. *bouwen*[9] MnDu. *bouwen* (cf. particularly *landbouwen* v.)[10] MnFris. *bouwe*[11] are all applied to the cultivation of land. The sentence *þa beormas hæfdon swiþe wel gebúd* (v.r. *gebún*) *hira land* is definitely in favour of the second possibility—that here *(ge)búan* means ' to cultivate ' for any translation taking the word as meaning ' to occupy ' would be forced. This view of *(ge)búan* as meaning ' to cultivate ' is strongly supported by the reference later in Ohthere's account to the cultivated areas on the west coast of Norway where *þæt byne land* ' the cultivated land ' is clearly equated to ' all of it [*sc.* the land] that can be grazed or ploughed.' It seems therefore that we must interpret *gebūn* as meaning ' cultivated,' not merely ' occupied ' and translate as on p. 19; Ohthere thus makes a sharp contrast between the well-cultivated land of the Beormas and the land of the Terfinnas which was *wēste*—this is presumably to be taken as meaning both uncultivated and without settled habitation.

The reference to agriculture[12] at such a latitude is of interest and it is unfortunate that we can know nothing of the details. At the present day—so Mr. A. Ph. Anisimov kindly informs me—the cultivation of rye, the ripening of fodder-grass and hay-making are possible on the south coast of the Kola Peninsula under natural conditions. We are however left in doubt as to whether the agriculture which Ohthere noticed was pastoral or arable or both; if arable, rye would seem to be the most probable crop, though (*teste* Professor J. Percival) barley is also conceivable.

[6] W. Müller and F. Zarncke, *Mittelhochdeutsches Wörterbuch* s.v. *Bûwe* II. 2. a.
[7] Grimm, *Deutsches Wörterbuch* s.v. *Bauen.*
[8] K. Schiller and A. Lübben, *Mittelniederdeutsches Wörterbuch* s.v. *Buwen* §2.
[9] E. Verwijs and J. Verdam, *Middelnederlandsch Woordenboek* s.v. *Bouwen* §2.
[10] *Woordenboek der nederlandsche taal* s.v. *Bouwen* III. iii. 1.
[11] W. Dijkstra, *Friesch woordenboek* s.v. *Bouwe.*
[12] On the value of the practice of agriculture among the Beormas as evidence for their identification see pp. 53, 57.

(iii) *Scandinavian-Bjarmian relations.* During a period which is usually regarded as extending from some time in the ninth century to about the year 1200 a number of Scandinavian expeditions went to Bjarmaland. The historical aspect of these expeditions has been sufficiently discussed elsewhere and the reader may be referred to the standard works *viz.* A. W. Brøgger " Håløygjenes Bjarmelandsferder " in *Festskrift til Rektor Qvigstad* (1928) also Chapter IV of the same author's *Nord-Norges Bosetningshistorie*; Tiander; H. Koht, " Gråfelden i norsk historie," *Norsk historisk tidsskrift* V. viii, 19-36.[13]

The Vikings must have found the ill-armed[14] Bjarmar an easy prey and apparently they established some kind of military supremacy over them.[15] The Bjarmian tax " viritim pellem pro capite " mentioned by Saxo 3 appears to be very similar to the Lappish tax referred to by Ohthere and to the *finnskattr* of Eg.s. chap. 17. One of the chief objects of these Viking expeditions was trading—chiefly for furs (Hkr 4, Qr.Os.).

We may appropriately conclude this section by discussing the last of all the mediaeval contacts between the Scandinavians and the Bjarmar : Flat. 4 tells us that King Hákon harboured many Bjarmar who had fled because of ' Tattar ' hostility and that he granted the Malangen Fjord to them.[16] The year was probably 1238 (Johnsen p. 21) and the obvious rendering of *Tattarar* is ' Mongols '—the passage thus being at first sight a reference to the Mongol penetration of Russia in the thirteenth century. But this interpretation

[13] Koht also discusses briefly the ousting of the Scandinavians by the Russians in this area; cf. Ld. fr. 2.
[14] Cf. the *kaupstefna* for weapons suggested by the Bjarmar in Qr. Os.
[15] Saxo's statement (6) that Regnerus engraved an inscription (presumably runic) on the rocks to commemorate his victory over the Bjarmar rings very true; runic inscriptions from the White Sea area may yet come to light.
[16] But a search for present-day evidence of a Bjarmian infusion in this area would be unprofitable for both the anthropological and the linguistic evidence must be masked by the (well-known) presence of Finns in this area (see A. Schreiner, *Die nord-norweger: anthropologische untersuchungen an soldaten* and O. Rygh, *Norske gaardnavne* vol. xvii: *Tromsø Amt*, p. vii).

presents difficulties. For Mongol penetration is not usually assumed to have extended nearly as far north as ' Bjarmaland ' (see, for example, K. V. Kudrjashov, *Russkij Istoricheskij Atlas*, Plate V; *Cambridge Medieval History* iv, Map 46). The prevailing view in the Russian literature of the subject[17]—which is apparently due to Tiander p. 439—is that *Tattarar* means here, not Mongols, but Russians from Novgorod.[18] This unduly simplifies the problem—and the suggestion that ' Mongols ' and ' Russians ' were synonymous terms tö the Bjarmar by reason of the fact that, by the middle of the thirteenth century, the Russians were already in subjection to the Golden Horde, hardly affords a way out of the difficulty either. The Norse reference must in fact be interpreted in the obvious way and *Tattarar* taken as ' Mongols.' For there is further evidence that the orthodox view as to the lack of Mongol penetration in the Dvina area must be revised. P. Savitskij, *Nauchnye trudy Russkago Narodnago Universiteta v Prage* v, 141 calls attention to John de Plano Carpini's[19] (1245-7) brief mention of a Mongol campaign against the Samoyedes.[20] Even assuming that the Samoyedes were no further south than they are to-day (see Sketch-Map), this affords clear evidence of Mongol pressure in an area not very far from the Dvina; it should also be remembered that the Samoyedes were probably the eastern neighbours of the

[17] See, most recently, V. Ju. Vize, *Morja Sovetskoi Arktiki* (1936) p. 12.
[18] This view is also accepted—tentatively—by Koht, *op. cit.* p. 31 note.
[19] Marco Polo (c. 1254-1324), in the fifty-sixth chapter of his first book (ed. of H. Yule, revised by H. Cordier, 1903), refers to a place on the ocean in the extreme north which was a breeding-ground for peregrine falcons. He says:—" And when you have travelled forty days over this great plain you come to the ocean, at the place where the mountains are in which the peregrine falcons have their nests . . . And when the Grand Kaan wants Peregrines from the nest, he sends thither to procure them. It is also on islands in that sea that the Gerfalcons are bred. You must know that the place is so far to the north that you leave the North star somewhat behind you towards the south ! " Savitskij, *loc. cit.*, points out that this can only be interpreted as referring to the point at which the Urals run down into the Arctic Ocean in the Pai-Khoi range (the islands might thus be Vaigach' and Novaja Zemlja) and would see in the passage another reference to Mongol suzerainty in the extreme north.
[20] See C. R. Beazley, *The texts and versions of John de Plano Carpini and William de Rubruquis*, p. 88.

Bjarmar (see p. 58). In a letter of 20/6/1937 Professor Savitskij kindly points out that the presence of Mongols in this area is further attested by the frequent references to Bugai (fl. c. 1262), a Mongol *bogatyr'* ('hero') of Velikij Ustjug, in Russian folk-literature.[21]

(iv) *The Bjarmar*. Of the life of the Bjarmar we learn next to nothing[22] and the discussion is here confined to two points:—

(A) *Religion*. We have considerable information as to the religious observances and, particularly, the burial rites of the Bjarmar. The best source is undoubtedly the very full description in Hkr. 4.[23] But the obviously romanticised accounts in Bósas. (both versions) and Sts.st. must also be considered in this connection. The discrimination between true and false however lies far outside the scope of the present monograph and must be left to the specialist in Finno-Ugrian religion.

But the mention of *Jomali*, the god of the Bjarmar, in Hkr. 4 and Bósas. is one of the most important points in the identification of the Bjarmar. The word is obviously very closely connected with Finn. *jumala* 'god'; since the word is native Finno-Ugrian, this one fact is sufficient to prove that the Dvina-Bjarmar were Finno-Ugrian. A more detailed discussion of the word follows (pp. 49-50).

(B) *Language*. Another very important point in the identification of the Bjarmar is Ohthere's definite statement that "it seemed to him that the Lapps and the Beormas spoke almost the same language." Ohthere had had many dealings with the Lapps and must have known what Lappish sounded like; it is indeed very probable that he spoke some Lappish himself. We thus have no reason to doubt the accuracy of his impression. Lappish is a Finno-Ugrian

---

[21] See particularly A. V. Ekzempljarskij, *Velikie i udel'nye knjaz'ja Severnoi Rusi v tatarskij period* ii, 75.

[22] The hall-scene in Qr. Os. is too similar to the typical Germanic description to be taken as specifically Bjarmian.

[23] Cf. also the mounds in Qr. Os. and Hálfss.

language and Ohthere's statement is alone sufficient to prove that his Beormas were Finno-Ugrian. A more detailed discussion follows (pp. 50-1).

From our consideration of the Scandinavian evidence we have thus reached certain definite conclusions as to the identification of the Bjarmar; these may be summarised as follows:—

(1) There were two parts of Bjarmaland : one in the Dvina-area, the other on the north side of Kandalaks Bay. The localisation of the first area is proved by actual references to the Dvina, that of the second by the position of Ohthere's *Beormas* near his *Terfinnas* (this proof is thus dependent upon the proof of the position of the *Terfinnas* which is, in turn, rendered certain by (a) Ohthere's log and (b) the localisation of the name *Ter-*).

(2) The inhabitants of both parts of Bjarmaland were Finno-Ugrian. For the Dvina-Bjarmar this is proved by the mention of their god Jomali, for Ohthere's *Beormas* by his statement that they spoke almost the same language as the Lapps.

I proceed to a more detailed discussion of the identification of the Bjarmar. Five different suggestions as to which of the Finno-Ugrian peoples the Bjarmar may have been have been made; *viz.* that they are (1) Lapps;[24] (2) Komi-Syryänes[25]—who together with the Udmurt-Votyaks form the Permian sub-group; (3) Baltic Fenns—either (a) Vatja-Vots,[26] (b) Veps[27] or (c) Karelians.[28]

I may first deal with two special pieces of linguistic evidence:—

(i) As has already been stated (p. 48) *Jomali*, the god of the Dvina-Bjarmar in Hkr. 4 and Bósas., clearly corresponds

[24] In the modern literature apparently only Vasmer IV, 259.
[25] Only in the antiquated literature—see the Preface.
[26] Only Jaakkola p. 273 ff.
[27] Borenius, *Suomen Kuvalehti* 1873, p. 272; and, as an alternative to Karelians, Tallgren.
[28] This is the prevailing view; e.g. that of M. A. Castrén, *Suomi* 1844, pp. 1-22; Wichmann p. 407; SS ii, 76-7; Johnsen p. 9.

to Finn. *jumala* 'god.' This word is found in Baltic Fennic (Finn. *jumala* Est. *jumal* Veps *jumā* Vatja *jumaλ* etc.) and Lappish:—Ter, Kil'din *jimmel* Inari *immel*, *ibmel* Norwegian Finmark *(j)ibmel* Frostvik, Offerdal Undersåker, Härjedalen *jippmɛlɛ* : Akkala *jummel* Lule *juppmēl* Arjeplog *upmēl* Malå *jubmel* Stensele *jupmele* Vilhelmina *juppmɛlɛ* (Wiklund p. 251). An identical form is not found elsewhere but cf. the related Mari *jɔˑmɔ*, *jùˑmɔ* 'God' Mordvin *jon*, *jondol*, *jondəl* 'lightning.'[29] The question whether OWN. *Jomali* could represent the protoform of Lappish forms such as Lule *juppmēl* (before the change of *a* to *e* in the second syllable in Lappish)[30] is very difficult. It will suffice to say here that, on philological grounds, this is somewhat unlikely for the Lappish variation in this word between forms with initial *ju* (some of which may be due to direct Finnish influence) and those with initial *(j)i* appears to be distributed so that the forms with *ju* are found in the Middle Lappish dialects, not in the Northern (and Russian Lappish) and Southern dialects; presumably it would be the Russian Lappish forms that would be important for our point. The word is not found in Komi so that the Dvina-Bjarmar can hardly have been Komi. The evidence of Jomali is thus in favour of the Dvina-Bjarmar being Baltic Fenns.[31]

(ii) Ohthere's statement that the Beormas spoke almost the same language as the Lapps makes it clear that they were not Komi. The Finno-Ugrian languages differ widely and, even at his date, it is out of the question that anyone should have described Komi as strikingly similar to Lappish. The statement would of course be readily intelligible if we assumed his Beormas to have been merely a tribe of Lapps. But it is as

[29] On the question whether Komi *jen* ' god ' Udmurt *in*, *i* ·, *im* ' heaven '; *inmar*, *iṅmar*, *immar* ' god ' Finn. *ilma* ' air, weather etc.'; *Ilmari(nen)* n.pr. Norwegian Lappish *albme* ' heaven ' Ostyak *(num)itəm*: *(num-īləm)* ' heaven, heavenly god '; *jilem*: *jilem-tut* ' Northern lights ' (lit. ' heavenly light ') Vogul *ēlem*, *ilem*, *jelem* ' weather ' belong here see Uotila p. 75 where further references will be found.
[30] P. Ravila, *Hirt-Festschrift* (1936) ii, 103.
[31] The details of the relationship between OWN. *Jomali* and the Baltic Fennic etymon are difficult; I discuss this question *Acta Philologica Scandinavica*, xi, 170-3.

intelligible if we take the Beormas as Baltic Fenns. Lappish is, in part, a form of Baltic Fennic (see below) and the further we go back the more striking will be the similarity between the two languages. Moreover the similarity due to this cause is enhanced by the large number of Finnish loan-words which, presumably ever since the 'language-shift' (see below), have passed in a steady stream into those Lappish dialects in contact with the Finns. In Ohthere's time the natural similarity between Baltic Fennic and Lappish must have been very striking and we may also suppose that already a considerable number of Baltic Fennic loan-words had been borrowed into Lappish.

Turning now to the five identifications suggested for the Bjarmar:—

I. *The Lapps*. The question of the position of Lappish within the Finno-Ugrian family is difficult. It is clear that the Lapps are related to the Finns in language, equally clear that they are unrelated in race. Presumably therefore the Lapps originally spoke a non-Finno-Ugrian language which we may conveniently call 'pre-Lappish.' In a recent article " Die stellung des lappischen innerhalb der finnisch-ugrischen sprachfamilie ", FUF. xxiii, 20-65, P. Ravila deals with the problem[32] and (p. 63) summarises his conclusions as follows:— " dass der wesentliche teil des lappischen teils aus einer vorfinnischen sprachform, die noch nach der trennung aller anderen finnisch-ugrischen sprachen vorhanden war, teils aus der schon deutlich urfinnischen sprachform hervorgegangen ist." We have of course no evidence as to when the Lappish 'language-shift' took place; presumably a very long time before Ohthere's voyage.

The distribution of the Lapps at the present day—in Lapland, also in parts of Sweden and Norway—is sufficiently indicated on the map. But formerly the Lapps were much more widely distributed than they are to-day, both in Finland

---

[32] See also P. Ravila, " Die Lappen und Fennoskandien," *Hirt-Festschrift* (1936) ii, 97-107.

and Russia. This is shown by actual references to Lapps and by Lappish place-names and loan-words. The former distribution in Finland does not concern us here,[33] but that postulated for Russia is very relevant to the present problem so far as the Dvina area is concerned. The Russian evidence forms the chief part (§§1-9) of Vasmer IV.[34] Vasmer first discusses (§6) the numerous references in the historical sources to the presence of Lapps in parts of Russia without Lapps to-day (e.g. in Povenets U.[35] of Olonets G. and around Lake Onega). He then proceeds (§8) to a detailed discussion of the place-names of Lappish origin in Russia; these he finds in:—Archangel G. : Kem' U., Archangel U., Kholmogory U., Onega U., Pinega U. (no definite evidence in Shenkursk U.); Olonets G. : Povenets U., Pudozh U., Petrozavodsk U., Olonets U., Kargopol' U., Vytegra U. (traces); Leningrad G. : Novaja-Ladoga U. (traces); Novgorod G. : Belozersk U., Kirilov U., Cherepovets U., Tikhvin U. His results for the position of the Lapps in Russia before his 'Baltic Fennic' and 'Russian' expansions are indicated on his map; I have inserted these entries on my Sketch-Map—they are followed by a (V.) and appear in green.

There are no actual references to Lapps on the Dvina but, while not admitting all Vasmer's place-name evidence without reserve, it must be said that he has produced sufficient to render the presence of Lapps near the mouth of the Dvina a possibility (cf. also p. 60) and we must therefore consider whether the Bjarmar may not have been Lapps. But with regard to the Dvina area it must be pointed out that an early date (as assumed by Vasmer) for all these supposed Lappish settlements in Russia is by no means assured. We know

---

[33] See K. B. Wiklund "Lapparnas forna utbredning i Finland och Ryssland, belyst af ortnamnen" *Le Monde oriental* v, 101-36; and, for Lappish loan-words in Finnish, F. Äimä, SUSA xxv, 1.

[34] For the Lappish loan-words in Russian see T. Itkonen in *Mikkola-Festschrift* (*Annales Academiae Scientiarum Fennicae*, vol. 27); reviewed by J. Kalima, FUF. xxiii, 247 ff.

[35] I follow Vasmer in his use of the classification by *gubernija* 'Government' (abbreviated G.) and *uezd* 'District' (abbreviated U.).

so little about the early history of the Lapps that we are in fact hardly in a position to decide with certainty whether, if there were Lapps in the Dvina area, these would represent an early settlement or a later immigration east. On the latter hypothesis we might perhaps consider that Lapps are not likely to have been in the Dvina area as early as the period of the Bjarmaland Voyages.

But, apart from this, the suggestion that the Bjarmar were Lapps appears improbable on general grounds. There is indeed nothing in the distribution of the Lapps to militate against the suggestion that Ohthere's *Beormas* on Kandalaks Bay were merely a tribe of Lapps slightly different from his *Terfinnas*. But this supposition is definitely disproved by Ohthere's reference to agriculture among the *Beormas*; for this has always been lacking in the economy of the Lapps. Moreover the Scandinavians (and Ohthere in particular) were thoroughly familiar with the Lapps; had the Bjarmar been Lapps we should expect the Scandinavians to have said so—they could hardly have been mistaken about a race so distinctive. Finally the evidence of *Jomali*, difficult though it is, would seem to be against the Dvina-Bjarmar being Lapps (see p. 50).

2. *The Komi.* The distribution of the Komi at the present-day—chiefly in the Governments of Vjatka, Vologda, Perm' and Archangel—is sufficiently indicated on the map; the present-day distribution of the closely-related Udmurt— chiefly in Vjatka G.—is also marked. But formerly the Komi apparently extended considerably further towards the White Sea (which alone concerns us here) than they do to-day, Vasmer IV §§10-14 deals with the place-name evidence for the one-time presence of Permians in territory which is no longer Permian. Most of his work does not directly concern us, for it deals with Permians in regions far south of that under discussion (e.g. Governments of Olonets, Novgorod, Vologda, Vjatka, Perm', Kazan', Kostroma). But the Permian material which he gives for Archangel G. is important from

our point of view since it clearly attests the one-time presence of Komi in this area; Permian material is found in this province in the Uezdy of Archangel, Kholmogory, Onega, Shenkursk, Pinega, Mezen' and Pechora. Vasmer's conclusions for his ' Permier ' (i.e., in the area under consideration, northern Permians, *that is* Komi) are indicated on his map and I have inserted them on mine (cf. p. 52 above).

It might thus be suggested that there were Komi at the mouth of the Dvina during the period of the Scandinavian-Bjarmian contacts. As evidence for the presence of Komi so far north one might adduce, first, the few Komi names on the White Sea e.g. *Jagry*, the name of two islands at the mouth of the Dvina (: Komi *jegyr* ' swamp, marshy ground ') given by Vasmer IV, 233; and secondly, the rather involved evidence of the loan-words of Komi. Of these it will suffice to say that Wichmann pp. 400-09 postulated a certain number of Karelian loan-words in Komi and assumed them to have been borrowed from the Karelian of the Dvina area. The same author also suggests, *Tietosanakirja* ix, 792, that there are even a few Norse loan-words in Komi. If either of these two suggestions of Wichmann's were accepted, some evidence for the early presence of Komi in this area would be afforded. As to the latter, Wichmann himself later considered it doubtful (p. 404) and Uotila, *Vir.* p. 203 note, rejects it; moreover, on the archæological side, Tallgren p. 107 points out that not a single Norse object—nor even an imitation of one—has hitherto been found among the rich and well-known Permian antiquities. Uotila *Vir.* considers the first suggestion in some detail; he comes to the conclusion that the Baltic Fennic loan-words in Komi may be either Karelian or Veps, the latter hypothesis being slightly the more probable. More important from our point of view, he considers that, having regard to the distribution of certain of the words in the Komi dialects, the point of contact between Komi and Baltic Fennic was probably somewhere in the region of the lower Vychegda, not the extreme north.

On examination therefore the evidence for the comparatively early presence of Komi on the shores of the White Sea is inconclusive and indeed neither Uotila *Vir.* p. 207 nor Vasmer IV (map) assumes it. It appears unlikely that the Komi can have reached the White Sea as early as the period of the first Bjarmaland journeys, considering that the end of the Primitive Permian period—in which the Komi and Udmurt were united under Bulgar Turk dominion—cannot have antedated them by long.[36] On general grounds, therefore, the Dvina Bjarmar cannot have been Komi; moreover conclusive evidence that they were not is afforded by the mention of *Jomali* (see p. 50). There is further no trace of Komi in the Kola Peninsula and consequently Ohthere's *Beormas* cannot have been Komi; this is also proved by his statement as to the language of the Beormas (p. 50). The identification of the Bjarmar as Komi is thus quite impossible.

3a. *The Vatja*. The present situation—near Leningrad—of the Vatja (even before the Great War only about a thousand in number) is sufficiently indicated on the Sketch-Map. Jaakkola's ill-advised suggestion that the Bjarmar were Vatja may be dismissed out of hand; though the Vatja were certainly more widely extended than they are to-day (SS ii, 115-21) there is no evidence whatsoever for so northerly a position at any date.

3b. *The Veps*. The present situation—chiefly between L. Ladoga and L. Onega—of the Veps (some 25,000 in number) is sufficiently indicated on the Sketch-Map. Very little is known of the early history of the Veps though their name is often mentioned (cf. Adam of Bremen's *Wizzi*,[37] (*V*)*īsū* in the Muslim sources,[38] ORuss. *Vesb*).[39] There is however no evidence at all for the presence of Veps in the far north. It

---

[36] Y. Wichmann SS ii, 313—and see also his *Die tschuwassischen Lehnwörter in den permischen Sprachen* p. 140 ff.—concludes that the Primitive Permian period was at an end by the eleventh century.
[37] Descriptio Insularum Aquilonis §14 (G. H. Pertz, *Monumenta Germaniae Historica*: *Scriptorum* vii, 373 line 17).
[38] See V. Minorsky, *Hudūd al-ʿAlam* p. 437.
[39] See SS ii, 110-11.

should be noted here that Uotila *Vir.* p. 207 would explain his Veps-Komi contacts in the Vychegda area as due, not to any real spread of Veps, but merely to the presence of isolated colonists. The suggestion that the Bjarmar were Veps can therefore be dismissed.

3c. *The Karelians.* The present situation of the Karelians—in the territory just east of the former Finnish-Soviet frontier—is sufficiently indicated on the Sketch-Map. The Karelians may be divided into a south and a north branch and it is with the latter that we are concerned. The one-time presence of Karelians in the White Sea area is well-attested by a number of names containing the word ' Karelian ' in parts no longer Karelian-speaking. Thus Vasmer II, 412 mentions from Archangel G. names such as *Korel'skoje* (Onega U.), *Bol'shaja* and *Malaja Korel'skaja* (Archangel U.), *Korel'skaja Gora* (Pinega U.)[40] and further certain older names *viz.* (i) *Korel'skij bereg* ' the shore of the White Sea from the mouth of the Dvina west to the R. Njukhcha '; (ii) *Korel'skoje Ust'je* (XVI-XVII cent.) ' a channel of the Dvina '; (iii) *Shuja Korel'skaja* (XVI cent.) ' a river that flows into the White Sea between the R. Kem' and the R. Vyg '; (iv) he refers to the Chronicle of Novgorod *s.a.* 1419; the Synodal Transcript[41] mentions here . . . . . *vъ Arzugi pogostъ Korilъskyi* ' Karelian parishes in [the district of] Arzuga [*i.e.* Varzuga]'.[42]

It is furthermore probable that the ORuss. *Zavolochъskaja Chudъ* (i.e. the *Chudъ* ' Finns,' *za* ' at the back of,' *volok* ' the portage *or* watershed between the Dvina and the

---

[40] Wichmann, p. 407, takes the first element of Komi *Kar-dor* ' Archangel ' as meaning ' Karelian ' but Uotila *Vir.* p. 204 rejects this suggestion.

[41] *Novgorodskaja Letopis po Sinodalnomu Kharatsinomu Spisku* (*Izd. Arkheograficheskoi Komissii*, 1888) p. 409.

[42] See also Vasmer IV, 186 where some further interesting references for the Karelian name in this area are given, *viz.* (i) 15th century references (not quoted but citing E. K. Ogorodnikov, *Zapiski imperatorskago russkago geograficheskago obshchestva po otdelniju etnografii* ii, 612); (ii) the " *Korel'skij Nikolajevskij Monastyr'* "; (iii) the general name *korel'skije deti* ' Karelian children ' used of the Karelians in this area.

Volga '), to whom there are many references, are the Northern Karelians (see SS ii, 75), though (see p. 7) I must refrain from any discussion of this question here.

In this connection it may be noted that Vasmer II deals with the place-name evidence for the one-time presence of Baltic Fenns in the non-Karelian-speaking parts of Archangel G. (p. 412 ff.);[43] he finds plentiful evidence for Baltic Fennic nomenclature in the various Uezdy—in Kem' U., Onega U., and, of particular interest to us, in Archangel U., Kholmogory U. and Pinega U. (while in Shenkursk U. and Mezen' U. definite evidence appears to be lacking). This Baltic Fennic material can only be interpreted as Karelian— for neither the Vatja nor the Veps (nor any other Baltic Fennic tribe) can be assumed for this area—and therefore affords strong evidence in support of that of the Karelian name mentioned above.

And this view of the presence of Karelians in the area under consideration is strongly reinforced by the archæological evidence. According to Tallgren p. 111 ff. the finds of extreme north Russia of about 1000 A.D., though showing Permian influence, are connected primarily with the Ladoga area and are thus Karelian or Veps (this latter possibility we have rejected on other grounds).

It is thus very probable that there were Karelians in the White Sea area at the time of the Bjarmaland Voyages and the Dvina Bjarmar were in all probability Karelians; these fulfil the necessary conditions of situation and worship of *Jumala*. It is then probable that Ohthere's *Beormas* were also Karelians; this assumption would explain the close similarity between the language of the *Terfinnas* and the *Beormas* (see pp. 50-1) and, since agriculture is an essential element in Karelian economy (SS ii, 42 ff.), it is also consistent with Ohthere's reference to agriculture among the Beormas. Moreover good evidence for the one-time presence of Karelians

[43] The rest of the work does not in general concern us for it deals with regions far south (e.g. Governments of Pskov, Tver', Novgorod, etc.).

on the Varzuga (perhaps the very river up which Ohthere sailed—see p. 24) is afforded by the mention of the ' Karelian parishes ' there in 1419 (see p. 56).

Summarising it may be said that the suggestions that the Bjarmar were Vatja, Veps or Komi are very improbable; that they were Lapps, improbable; but that they were Karelians, very probable.[44]

From the point of view of the Scandinavians we may thus envisage the two parts of Bjarmaland as Karelian territories in which on the one hand the Dvina and, on the other, either the Umba or the Varzuga were situated. The question whether the two parts of Bjarmaland adjoined naturally arises; and, with a strong degree of probability, it may at once be answered in the affirmative. It is in fact very probable that the Karelian population stretched right round the shores of the White Sea; at one end of the circle the extreme limit may perhaps be taken as the Pinega (Vasmer II, 424);[45] from here the territory extended past the mouth of the Dvina, along the southern shore of the White Sea, and finally, round the head of Kandalaks Bay. On the extreme east the Karelian territory must have adjoined that of the Samoyedes, while the limit of eastern penetration into Lappish territory in the Kola Peninsula at the time of Ohthere would appear to be laid down by his statement " on the other [i.e. the western] side of the river the land was thoroughly cultivated "; we may thus take Ohthere's river (either the Varzuga or the Umba) as the then Karelian-Lappish frontier. Tallgren p. 118 wishes to put the southern limit of Bjarmaland as far south as L.Ladoga, his arguments being chiefly based on the position indicated in Hfds.Ey. and on the statement

[44] Our conclusion that the Bjarmar were essentially Karelians does not of course preclude the possibility of there being minor elements in the population of Bjarmaland; there may have been a few Lapps, and possibly—at any rate by the time of the later Bjarmaland Voyages—even a few Komi traders.

[45] The most easterly find that is certainly Karelian would appear to be a find—of about the time of the Crusades—at Vaimushe on the Pinega (Tallgren p. 116). The find on the Usa, a tributary of the Pechora, appears too uncertain to be used as evidence for such a distant eastern limit (Tallgren pp. 116-7).

in Ld.fr. 1 that the two Cwen-lands are north of Bjarmaland (he would also interpret " Olaus Magnus on ' Hither ' and ' Further Biarmia ' " as further evidence—but on this see p. 43). His view may be correct. It seems however more probable that, to most Scandinavians, Bjarmaland was primarily a coastal region with a hinterland only vaguely conceived.

III. RUSSIAN *PERM'*.

The name *Per(e)m'* was apparently applied in three different ways in Old Russian:—(1) *Kolo-Perem'*, the western part of the Kola Peninsula (SS ii, 75; Johnsen p. 20, note 69) and thus presumably the territory of the Karelians; (2) Old *Perm'*, the territory of the Komi of the Vychegda and its tributaries the Vym' and the Sysola (SS ii, 346); (3) Great *Perm'*, the territory of the Komi of the Kama district (chief town Cherdyn')—SS ii, 347.[46] In modern Russian the Komi of the Governments of Perm' and Vjatka are called *permjaki* while those further north are called *zyrjáne*[47] (hence German *syrjänisch* etc.); in earlier Russian we also find the names *perm'*, *permjáne*, *permíchi* for the Komi (SS ii, 332-3).

OWN. *Bjarmar* and ORuss. *Per(e)m'* are obviously closely related, but, whereas in OWN. the name was applied to Karelians, in Russian it was used both of their territory (*Kolo-Perem'*) and of that of the Komi (Old *Perm'* and Great *Perm'*). I give a detailed discussion of the relationship between the Scandinavian and Russian forms LSE. vi, 5-13.

IV. THE MUSLIM SOURCES.

The Scandinavian and Russian sources are the only ones of any real value for the early historical geography of the White Sea area. With regard to the Chinese sources it may be said that these certainly contain some references to Siberia; it is however unlikely that they reach as far west as the White Sea; in any case they have never been properly investigated.

[46] Hence the name of the modern Government of Perm'.
[47] Probably from the Vogul name for the Komi *saran*.

It is possible that the Muslim geographers had some information—of a very vague kind—about the White Sea area. Thus J. Markwart in his article " Ein arabischer Bericht über die arktischen (uralischen) Länder aus dem 10. Jahrhundert," *Ungarische Jahrbücher* iv, 261-334 (especially p. 310 ff.) would interpret a difficult section (his §§12-14) in 'Aufī dealing with a seafaring people living, on the coast, on the far side of the *Jūra* (i.e. Jugra) as referring to Lapps at the mouth of the Dvina (see p. 52). In the *Taḥdīd al-amākin* written in 1025 (still unpublished) Bīrūnī mentions a voyage made by a *warang* ' Varangian ' in the Polar Regions; in his article " Die nordvölker bei Bīrūnī," *Zeitschrift der deutschen morgenländischen Gesellschaft* xc, 38-51, A. Zeki Validi suggests (pp. 47-8) that this is a reference to Ohthere's actual voyage. Iṣṭakhrī describes three kinds (*ṣinf*) of Rūs; two are probably to be identified as the people of Kiev and Novgorod; the third group are the *Arthāniya* whose king resides at *Arthā*. For the last two names there are many variant readings; *Arthā* is usually taken as equivalent to Mordvin *Er'z'a*, the name by which one of the branches of this people call themselves (SS ii, 269 ff.); but the (doubtful) variant reading *Ab.rqā* has been taken as *Abārma and identified with Biarmia by Khvol'son, *Izvestija ibn-Dasta* p. 174 ff., who however rather vitiates his suggestion by taking Biarmia to be the same as Perm' (see p. 5); a more correct localisation of Biarmia would in fact militate against this view for a location of *Abārma on the White Sea would certainly conflict with this part of the geography of Iṣṭakhrī; see also V. Minorsky, *Ḥudūd al-'Alam* p. 436 note 2. Finally I may mention that O. J. Tuulio (Tallgren), *Du nouveau sur Idrīsī* p. 170 ff. would find a reference to Biarmia in Idrīsī. The form under discussion occurs in the text of Climate VI, Section 5 and in the Maps—in the extreme north-east of the map in VII. 5 (consequently also in the extreme north-west of that in VII. 6).[48] In VI. 5, A. Jaubert's

[48] See Tuulio's Plates 4, 17 and Map II.

translation[49] reads:—"Six grandes rivières mêlent leurs eaux à celles du fleuve de Russie [*rwsyh, rwšyh*] . . . dont les sources sont dans les montaignes de Cocaïa *qwf'y'*,[50] qui s'étendent depuis la mer Ténébreuse jusqu'aux extrémités du monde habité . . . Elles sont inaccessibles, à cause de l'excès du froid et de la permanence des neiges sur leurs sommets. Les vallées sont habitées par les peuples dits Nibaria *nb'ry^t*." The maps used by Tuulio have *nb'ryh* (or *bn'yrh*—the pointing is ambiguous) and *m'ryh*; he would regard all the forms as due ultimately to corruption of *by'rmh i.e. *Bi'ārma or *Biyārma.[51]

---

[49] A. Jaubert, *Géographie d'Edrisi* ii, 396.
[50] i.e. the 'Ριπαια of the Greeks (see Tuulio, *loc. cit.*).
[51] If Tuulio's view be accepted I may point out the similarity between the above passage in Idrisi and Saxo 5.

ADDITIONAL NOTE (1940)

ADDITIONAL NOTE.

This monograph has been a long time in the press and the following additional literature now calls for mention. (I) V. Jansson, Bjarmaland, *Ortnamnssällskapets i Uppsala årsskrift* i, 33-50 (I am indebted to Dr. A. H. Smith, London, for calling my attention to this interesting article). Jansson briefly enumerates the sources (on p. 40 he shows that the influence of Olaus Magnus' *Biarmia* on cartography extends even later than Ahlenius supposed [see p. 42], the entry continuing right down to the eighteenth century); he then refers briefly to the literature of the subject. There then follows the original part of the article: Jansson calls attention to certain place-names in Norway and Sweden and suggests a new etymology for *Bjarmar*. The first of these place-names is most interesting—*Bjermeland* in Norway (Sylte Herred, Romsdal Amt), recorded in 1430-40 (*af Biarmalande*); Jansson is certainly right in suggesting that this was named directly from the real Bjarmaland. He then mentions *Bjørlien* in Norway (*Biermelijdh* in 1543) and various names in Sweden all containing the first element *Bjärm-* viz. *Bjärme* (cf. early forms such as *Biærmo*, 15th century), *Bjärmegården*, *Bjärmsjön*, *Bjärmtjärn*, *Bjärmsnäs*. From a consideration of the topography of some of these places he suggests that an ON. stem *biarm-* meaning 'height, mountain' underlies them and that *Bjarmaland* is to be explained as containing the same stem. He finally suggests that this ON. *biarm-* represents a PrGmc. *$\beta\epsilon\rho\gamma$-ma-* or *$\beta\epsilon\rho\gamma ama$-*, related to MnHG. *berg*, etc., and to be equated to the Celtic place-name *Bergamo* in Italy (for the early forms see A. Holder, *Alt-celtischer Sprachschatz* s.v. *Berg-omo-n*) which, according to P. Kretschmer, *Glotta* xxii, 113 ff., is the same as Greek Πέργαμος. With regard to the morphology he would derive OWN. *Bjarmar* from PrGmc. *$\beta\epsilon\rho\gamma(a)man$-* and OSw. *Biærmo* (MnSw. *Bjärme*) from PrGmc. *βerγ(a)mō(n-. I do not find Jansson's etymology convincing but it is certainly possible that his names in *Bjärm-* are related to *Bjarmaland*, in which case I would suggest that they be derived from one or more of the stems discussed by me LSE vi, 11—IndE. *bhermŏ-, *bhermā-; for the sense we might then well compare words such as Serbo-Croat *brdo* ' mountain, hill.' (II). R. Hennig, *Terrae Incognitae* ii, 186-98, gives a German translation and a discussion of Ohthere's Voyage; there is however much to criticise. (III). E. Kvalen, *The early Norwegian settlements on the Volga*. This book cannot be regarded as a serious contribution to the subject and the acrimonious tone in which it is written does not dispose one to devote space to discussing it. (IV) M. Zsirai in his *Finnugor Rokonságunk* [Our Finno-Ugrian relationship] devotes considerable space to Ohthere (pp. 204, 423 and particularly 472 ff.); he adds nothing new and his treatment is open to criticism; see further my review, *Journal of the Royal Asiatic Society* 1939, p. 443 ff. (V) In *Saga-Book of the Viking Society* xii, 15 I have called attention to the fact that ON. *jalda* ' mare ' < *elda* < *elða* < Finn. *älðä* (=Mordvin *äl'd'ä*, *el'd'e* ' mare ' Lapp. *al'do* ' reindeer-cow ') affords an interesting morphological parallel to OWN. *Jomali* < ONKar. *jumala* (=Finn. *jumala*) ' god ' [see p. 50]. (VI). I have also now had access to the printed versions of the Huldarsaga. There is no mention of Bjarmaland in the shorter one (*Sagan af Huld hinni miklu og fjölkunnugu trölldrotningu*, Akureyri, 1911—of which there is a copy in the Royal Library, Copenhagen). But in the longer version (*Sagan af Huld drottningu hinni ríku*, Reykjavik, 1909) there are references to Bjarmaland. Lack of space prevents me from summarising them here—they are of a highly fantastic character.

ADDITIONAL NOTE (1978)

Bjarmian Names in Literary Tradition

As I have shown in my monograph reprinted above (hereinafter cited as *Ohthere*), the Bjarmar were Karelians. The names assigned to them in literary tradition are, however, Scandinavian: *Ljúfvina* (L),[1] daughter of the King of the Bjarmar, Landnámabók (*Ohthere* p. 31); *Heiðr* (L), who dwelt on Gandvik—for this place-name, see below—Flateyjarbók (*Ohthere* p. 32); *Hárekr* (L), King of the Bjarmar, and his mother *Kolfrosta* (L); also a Bjarmian called *Hóketill* (L), Bósa saga (*Ohthere* p. 34); *Óttarr* (L), King of the Bjarmar, Hálfdanar saga Brǫnufóstra (*Ohthere* p. 35); *Rǫndólfr* (L), King of the Bjarmar, and a woman called *Guðríðr* (L *Guðriðr*), Sturlaugs saga Starfsama (*Ohthere* pp. 36-7). In the Hálfdanar saga Eysteinssonar there are many Bjarmian names: the King, *Hárekr* (L); his daughter, *Eðný* (L); his nephews *Valr* (L) (with sons *Kǫttr* (L) and *Kisi* (L)[2]) and *Ragnarr* (L) (with son *Agnarr* (L)). In the doubtless postmedieval Sagan af Huld drottningu hinni ríku (Reykjavík, 1909) we have "Arnfinnur (L) er maður nefndur ... hann bjó þar er í Vogum heitir, norður af Finnmörk, og inn af þeim hafsbotni, er Gandvík heitir. Hann var sonur Atla (L) sterka Eyvindssonar (L) kleggja, og Alvarar (L) dóttur Þryms (L) konungs, en hann var sagður sonur Snæs (L) konungs hins gamla. Arnfinnur átti Berghildi (L) ... þau Arnfinnur bjuggu að bæ þeim, er að Gerpi heitir. Þau áttu dóttur eina barna er Herríður (L) hét" (pp. 41-2). Bjarmians are also mentioned in Saxo. There is *Egtherus* (L *Eggþér*), King of the Bjarmar; *Guthmundus* (L *Guðmundr*) and his brother *Geruthus* (L *Geirrøðr*) appear to be Bjarmar; and

---

[1] An L after a name refers to E. H. Lind, *Norsk-isländska dopnamn ock fingerade namn från medeltiden* (1905-31); I give the head-word only if this differs from the form in the text—differences due to flexion are not taken account of; in one case an *L means that a name in Saxo is not paralleled in Lind.

[2] Admittedly *kissa* "cat" exists in Karelian, but this is a borrowing of Finn. *kissa*, which, in turn, is a borrowing of Swed. *kisse*; see Y. H. Toivonen, *Suomen kielen etymologinen sanakirja* I (1955), s.v. *kissa*.

Thuningus (v.r. *Turingus*) (*L), who collects a band of "Byarmenses", and *Guso* (L *Gusir*) ("Gusonis [v.r. Cusonis] Finnorum Byarmorumque principis") and his daughter *Thora* (L *Þóra*) may also be Bjarmar (*Ohthere* pp. 39-40).[3] These names, then, where identifiable, are Scandinavian. In the case of the romantic sagas it is easy to understand why they should be: the narrators did not know Karelian and had to use fabricated Scandinavian names. In the other material, it may be that some of the Bjarmar really did have Scandinavian names. *Ljúfvina* in Landnámabók sounds genuine; her naming is really no odder than that an English girl should be called *Yvonne*.

The name of the god of the Bjarmar, *Jomali*, is however Karelian; cf. my remarks *Ohthere* pp. 49-50, my article "Jomali", *Acta Philologica Scandinavica* XII, 170-3,[4] and the actual Karelian form *jumala* (= Finn. *jumala*), not cited by me. But in Sturlaugs saga Sturlaugr looks into a temple in Bjarmaland and sees Thor (*Ohthere* p. 36).

Apart from *Gandvík*, which I have discussed elsewhere,[5] we have no Bjarmian place-names except for three in the late Huldar saga, two already given and a further one in the passage: "Fyrir norðan Dumbshaf og Jötunheima liggur það land, er Bjarmaland heitir. Inn í það land liggur fjörður sá, er Skuggi heitir eða Skuggafjörður..." (*ed. cit.* pp. 49-50). *Í Vogum* (: OIcel. *vágr*) and *Skuggi* (: OIcel. *skuggi*) are clearly Scandinavian, and the third name, *að Gerpi*, is Scandinavian too: cf. *Gerpir*, a precipitous promontory in the middle of the east coast of Iceland.

[3] But *Hjálmarr* is not to be accepted as a Bjarmian name, for the "Historia Hialmari regis Biarmlandiæ atque Thulemarkiæ", published as *Fragmentum Mscr. Runici... Sub præsidio Joannis Bilberg...* Upsalæ, 1690 (see G. Hickes, *Linguarum vett. septentrionalium thesaurus grammaticocriticus et archæologicus: Dissertatio epistolaris*, 123 ff.), is a forgery: see H. Hermannsson, *Catalogue of the Icelandic Collection... in Cornell University Library* (1914), 245.

[4] The volume-number is wrongly given in the reference to this article at p. 50 note 31, above.

[5] "The place-name Kandalaksha", *Troisième congrès international de toponymie et d'anthroponymie*, ed. H. Draye and O. Jodogne, II-III: *Actes et mémoires* (1951), 429-32.

AFTERWORD

By Michael Chesnutt

In the forty years which have elapsed since Alan S. C. Ross published his monograph on Ohthere's voyage to the White Sea, Anglo-Saxonists have paid relatively little attention to the philological interpretation of the description of the voyage given in the Old English *Orosius*. Considerable advances have, however, been made with respect to the position of the *Orosius* translation within the framework of early West Saxon prose literature, and it is now possible to achieve a more precise understanding of the status of Ohthere's report as a historical source.

The great majority of earlier historians of Old English literature follow William of Malmesbury in attributing the *Orosius* translation to King Alfred the Great. This attribution implies the very highest degree of authority for the description of Ohthere's voyage, for the text we have represents Ohthere as personally informing King Alfred of his experiences in the remote North (cf. above, p. 16 line 1 = line 18, and p. 20 lines 3-4 = lines 7-8). It now seems, however, that the traditional inclusion of the *Orosius* among the works of Alfred must be abandoned: a number of scholars, commencing with Josef Raith in 1951, have demonstrated that the *Orosius* differs significantly in style from other texts which can be associated with the king on better evidence than that supplied by William of Malmesbury.[1] On the other hand, stylistic data are difficult to interpret in isolation, and it is certainly the case that the *Orosius* has much more in common with texts still generally admitted into the Alfredian corpus than with other Old English prose writings of the earlier period;[2]

---

[1] J. Raith, *Untersuchungen zum englischen Aspekt*, I. Teil (Studien und Texte zur Englischen Philologie I, 1951), 53-61; supplemented independently by Elizabeth M. Liggins, "The authorship of the Old English *Orosius*", *Anglia* LXXXVIII (1970), 289-322, and Janet M. Bately, "King Alfred and the Old English translation of Orosius", *ibid.* 433-60.

[2] Cf. Dorothy Whitelock, "The Prose of Alfred's Reign", *Continuations and Beginnings: Studies in Old English Literature*, ed. E. G. Stanley (1966), 67-103, at 89 and 93.

moreover, the Lauderdale manuscript of the *Orosius* (now British Library MS. Add. 47967), though not transcribed in the king's lifetime, is clearly a product of the tradition established at the West Saxon royal scriptorium by the last decade of the ninth century.[3] It is therefore entirely plausible that the account of Ohthere's voyage was derived from an official source at the court of Wessex—perhaps a memorandum of Ohthere's conversation with Alfred noted and preserved on a loose sheet in the royal archives. Since Raith not only found stylistic divergences between the main body of the *Orosius* translation and other works attributed to the king but also detected multiplicity of authorship in the geographical introduction containing the interpolations about Ohthere and Wulfstan,[4] it appears not unlikely that we owe our written record of Ohthere's activities to investigations made by an anonymous scholar at the court of Wessex, who was engaged in the translation of the Latin *Orosius*—or in the editing of an already existing translation—and who wished to supplement the geographical information given in his exemplar.

Such an explanation would weaken, though not necessarily wholly invalidate, the interpretation of the passage relating to Ohthere as a record composed or closely supervised by King Alfred himself. It would at all events imply the possibility that the transmitted text is not in every respect an accurate reproduction of Ohthere's report. Its kernel of historical truth

[3] See *The Tollemache Orosius*, ed. A. Campbell (Early English Manuscripts in Facsimile III, 1953), introduction, 16-17; N. R. Ker, *Catalogue of Manuscripts containing Anglo-Saxon* (1957), 164-6, no. 133; and A. Campbell, *Old English Grammar* (1959), 8-9, § 16.

[4] "Ich halte es für ausgeschlossen, daß Alfred die geschichtlichen Teile des Orosius übersetzt hat; zwischen Orosius einerseits, Boethius und Augustinus anderseits gähnt eine sprachliche Kluft, die schwer zu überbrücken sein durfte. Bei der geographischen Einleitung sind zweifellos mehrere Hände am Werk gewesen: die Reiseberichte Ohtheres und Wulfstans sind augenscheinlich von verschiedenen Leuten aufgezeichnet worden ... Die beiden Reiseberichte zeugen weder für noch gegen Alfred; aus der unpersönlichen Fassung (*Ohthere sæde his hlaforde Ælfrede cyninge*) lassen sich keine Schlüsse ziehen ..." (Raith [1951], 60-1).—As Raith remarks, distinctive linguistic features of the account of Wulfstan's voyage as compared with the preceding passage about Ohthere were already identified by W. A. Craigie, "The nationality of King Alfred's Wulfstan", *JEGP* XXIV (1925), 396-7.

may have been overlaid with distortions due to linguistic incomprehension and/or learned editing: it would be relevant here that René Derolez, in dealing with the long-standing issue of "shifted orientation" in the OE. *Orosius*, has suggested that the redactor adjusted his terminology in order to conform with the evidence of contemporary maps.[5]

My own view is that the manuscript tradition should not be treated with such exaggerated respect as to be confused with a stenographic record of an audience at the court of King Alfred.[6] It is accordingly inappropriate to attribute decisive importance to minor linguistic irregularities such as the monosyllabic first element in *Ter-finnas* (cf. above, pp. 27-8) or to the precise details of Ohthere's log with regard to duration of sailing or points of the compass. At the same time, there is no need to question the general historical reliability of Ohthere's narrative: on the contrary, everything tends to confirm that the text is a remarkably good paraphrase of what a ninth-century Norwegian might have said. Alan Binns has argued that Ohthere's sailing directions reflect the conscious choices of a skilled navigator who was intimately acquainted with the climatic conditions prevailing in the area between his home (perhaps at Senja) in North Norway and the Kola Peninsula at the entrance to the White Sea. The sequence of winds described is such as

[5] R. Derolez, "The orientation system in the Old English Orosius", *England before the Conquest: Studies in Primary Sources presented to Dorothy Whitelock*, ed. P. Clemoes and K. Hughes (1971), 253-68. For Latin texts as a source of supplementary geographical information see *inter alia* Janet M. Bately, "The relationship between geographical information in the Old English Orosius and Latin texts other than Orosius", *Anglo-Saxon England* I (1972), 45-62. The problem of orientation is further discussed on pp. 80-1 below.

[6] This formulation is of course wholly without prejudice to the question of whether the extant copies of the OE. *Orosius* are the (indirect) product of dictation in the scriptorium, on which see Janet M. Bately, "The Old English Orosius: the question of dictation", *Anglia* LXXXIV (1966), 255-304. She argues for dictation "by a Welshman of Latin education to a scribe with an Anglo-Saxon background" (304) as an explanation of abnormal spellings in the *Orosius* proper, and remarks that the Ohthere and Wulfstan passages "could have been composed by any one with connections with Alfred's court ... and could indeed have been added after the completion of the translation" (303 note 291).

would be necessary to ensure a good passage without excessive risk of storms: this is the technical motivation for Ohthere's otherwise unexplained delay at the northernmost tip of Norway (above, p. 16 lines 15-16 = lines 32-3), for Arctic trawlermen of the twentieth century report that depressions of the type which must have carried Ohthere's ship to North Cape tend to blow themselves out from the North-West, and a cautious skipper would accordingly wait until the wind had settled from that direction before proceeding East along the inhospitable Arctic coast.[7] As to the material purpose of his expeditions to the White Sea, his remark to the effect that walrus hides are good for making rope (above, p. 20 lines 1-4 = lines 5-8) is echoed in the thirteenth-century Norwegian *Konungs skuggsiá*,[8] and the place-name *Morzhovets* "Walrus Island" at the entrance to the White Sea is a modern testimony to the reality behind his description.[9] Even the idiom of Old Norwegian seems to be imitated on occasion: Ohthere's curious comment, found in two places, that the land curved away or *the sea entered the land*, he did not know which (above, p. 16 lines 14-15 = lines 30-2, and p. 18 lines 1-2 = lines 18-19), is reminiscent of the OIcel. expression *fjǫrðr skarsk inn í landit*.[10]

The most important question in which we are dependent upon the fidelity of the West Saxon writer toward his Norwegian informant is, of course, that of the ethnographic information about the peoples whom the Norwegian visitors encountered in the vicinity of the Kola Peninsula, the *Terfinnas* and the *Beormas*;

[7] Binns (1961), 44-7. (For abbreviated references see below, pp. 84-5.)
[8] Ed. Ludvig Holm-Olsen (Gammelnorske tekster utgitt av Norsk Historisk Kjeldeskrift-Institutt i samarbeid med Gammelnorsk Ordboksverk I, 1945), 29 lines 9-11: "huð hans er goð oc þiucc til reipa oc rista mænn þar af stærcar alar sva at væl draga sæx tigi manna æitt reip eða fleiri oc geta þo æigi slitit" (referring to the *rostongr*).
[9] Ekblom (1960), 9 (and cf. the map at 4, letter M).—For an eleventh-century Hispano-Arabic geographer's description of whaling as a parallel to Ohthere's reference to the catching of larger whales in his home territory (above, p. 20 lines 10-13) see Beatrice White, "Whale-hunting, The Barnacle Goose, and the Date of the 'Ancrene Riwle': Three Notes on Old and Middle English", *Modern Language Review* XL (1945), 205-7, at 205.
[10] Cf. Johan Fritzner, *Ordbog over Det gamle norske Sprog*[2] (1883-96), s.v. *skera* 11.

and here Ross's principal results appear to have stood the test of time. The etymological and ethnic identification of the *Terfinnas* as Lapps of the Kola Peninsula, a theory which originated with J. A. Sjögren (cf. above, p. 25), is as far as I can see quite satisfactory: in particular, the philological developments of the theory by Max Vasmer and Ross (above, pp. 25-7) dispose of all substantial difficulties regarding the related forms in Modern Russian, Finnish and Lappish. OE. *Ter-* < ON. **Ter-* as a substitution for PrLapp. **Târ-* (with "back" *i*) is perhaps the more attractive of the two alternatives admitted by Ross (p. 27) in explanation of the vocalism; but as I have already remarked, too much weight should not in any case be placed on the details of the West Saxon manuscript tradition.

The *Beormas* (ON. *Bjarmar*) are unfortunately more problematic. As far as the etymology and application of their name is concerned, two major schools of thought exist: the older, which can be traced back to Ph. von Strahlenberg in the early eighteenth century,[11] holds that the *Bjarmaland* of Norse tradition is historically related to Russ. *Perm'*, thus implying an etymological connection between the Germanic and Slavic nameforms, while the younger denies any historical relationship between *Bjarmaland* and *Perm'* and therefore eliminates the need for a philological explanation of the (apparent) similarity of nomenclature. This latter school is represented from the historical point of view by the Russian scholar Kuznetsov and others;[12] its most extreme proponent in the question of etymology is Valter Jansson, who proposes a purely Germanic background for the name *Beormas/Bjarmar* and holds Russ. *Perm'* to be of quite different derivation. In Jansson's opinion the Norse name contains a stem **biarm-* signifying some kind of high ground; *Bjarmaland, Bjarmar* would thus be descriptive names which were applied by Norse travellers like Ohthere to the territory and people that they encountered on their earliest expeditions to the White Sea, and would preserve the immediate physical impression

[11] Cf. Valter Jansson, "Bjarmaland", *Ortnamnssällskapets i Uppsala årsskrift* I:1 (1936), 33-50 (summarised above, pp. 62-3), at 42-3.
[12] See *inter alia* Koutaissoff (1948-49), summarising S. K. Kuznetsov, "K voprosu o Biarmii", *Etnograficheskoe Obozrenie*, LXV-VI (1905), 1-95.

made upon the Norsemen by the territory in question. A possible—though by no means certain—location of the earliest Norse/Bjarmian contacts would then be the district of Kholmogory on the Northern Dvina, for the name *Kholmogory* (older *Kalmakari*) has been explained from Finnish as meaning "mountain of the dead".[13]

Ross adopts an intermediate position between the two tendencies outlined above. In a paper published the year after Jansson's he arrives independently at a Germanic etymology for the names *Beormas/Bjarmar, Bjarmaland*: behind them lies an early Norse **Bjarm(r)* signifying "edge, shore" (cf. Mn Du. *berm*, E. *brim*, etc.). The Norse name is, however, definitely related to Russ. *Perm'*, having passed from Norse into Russian by way of Karelian.[14] This last assumption is a corollary of the ethnic identification of the *Beormas/Bjarmar* to which Ross lends his support, namely that they were Old Northern Karelians inhabiting the White Sea coast immediately to the South of the Kola Lapps (cf. above, pp. 56-8). There is no doubt that such a Karelian identification now constitutes the *communis opinio* among archaeologists and philologists,[15] the only significant voice of dissent being that of Vasmer, whose place-name studies convinced him that the *Beormas/Bjarmar* were Old Permians (Zyrians, Komi), though the name as applied by Ohthere to people living in the Kandalaks Bay vicinity must have referred to some Eastern Lappish tribe. (For objections to Vasmer's arguments see however above, pp. 53-5.)

As to the proposal of a native Norse origin for the name applied to this local population on the White Sea coast, the reasoning of Jansson proceeds from the observation that it was not wholly uncommon for the Norsemen to bestow their own names on

---

[13] Jansson (as note 11), 49-50.
[14] A. S. C. Ross, "OWN. *Bjarmar*: Russian *Perm'*", *Leeds Studies in English and Kindred Languages* VI (1937), 5-13 (cf. above, pp. 7 and 59).— For the representation of the Norse form as *Beormas* in Old English see Ross's paper on "Old Norse diphthongs in English", *Acta Philologica Scandinavica* XIV (1939-40), 1-10.
[15] See for example Tallgren (reference above, p. 12), 117-8; Jansson (as note 11), 45; Ekblom (1941-42), 137-8; Vilkuna (1956), 648.

Arctic peoples and places. He mentions the Norse appellation for the Lapps (*Finnar*) and other names of Nordic appearance associated in early texts with the White Sea area (*Vegistafr, Straumneskinnr* and *Gandvík*: on this last name, which Jansson considers "obviously Nordic at least in this form", see the discussion below).[16] Ross goes a stage further in supposing that the Bjarmians—having become acquainted with the terminology of their Norse visitors—"took over the name **Bjarm(r)*... for their own country".[17] His position is apparently unambiguous with respect to the later history of this allegedly Norse word: it was adopted by the Russians from the Northern Karelians as a designation for the territory of the latter, and subsequently transferred to the inland territories of the Old Permians. Cf. above, p. 59:

> OWN. *Bjarmar* and ORuss. *Per(e)m'* are obviously closely related, but, whereas in OWN. the name was applied to Karelians, in Russian it was used both of their [i.e. the Karelians'] territory (*Kolo-Perem'*) [an Old Russian name for part of the Kola Peninsula] and of that of the Komi (Old *Perm'* and Great *Perm'*).

This exposition does not tell us why the Russians should have felt it appropriate to transfer the name of one people to another, a point to which we must return.

Ross's own researches since the mid-1930s would in fact seem to swing the balance of probability away from the hypothesis that the Norsemen gave a name of their own invention to the Bjarmians. In the text of his monograph (see above, especially pp. 49-50) and in a separate article published in *Acta Philologica Scandinavica*[18] he had already treated the word *Jomali*, which is applied in saga texts to the god of the Bjarmians, as a Baltic Fennic loanword in Old Norse; and in 1941 he published a note in which he explains the Bjarmian river-name *Vína*, attested before A.D. 1000 in the *Gráfeldardrápa* of Glúmr Geirason (above, p. 29), as a reflex of an Old Northern Karelian name, **Vīna*. The

---

[16] Jansson (as note 11), 47.
[17] Ross (as note 14), 12.
[18] A. S. C. Ross, "Jomali", *Acta Philologica Scandinavica* XII (1937-38), 170-3. This article appeared earlier but was written later than the text of the monograph.

river-name would in other words be of what Ross calls "proximate Bjarmian" derivation, and he adds that "on *a priori* grounds this is the obvious suggestion, for it is reasonable to assume that the Scandinavians took the name of a Bjarmian river from the Bjarmar themselves".[19]

Is it, however, "reasonable to assume" that the Scandinavians would borrow a local (river-)name from a people on whom they themselves conferred an ethnic-territorial designation which that people adopted? A decade after his contribution on the Bjarmian *Vína* Ross propounded a new etymology for *Gandvík*, the sagas' name for the White Sea, arguing that the first element is a reflex of a Baltic Fennic parent-form **kanðan-* also seen in *Kantalahti/Kantalaksi*, the modern Finnish-Karelian appellation for Kandalaks Bay on the south side of the Kola Peninsula (cf. above, p. 24). With respect to the broader geographical application of *Gandvík* he writes:

> *Gandvík* is obviously the same name as *Kantalahti* but its geographical application is a little different. *Gandvík* evidently meant, primarily, 'the White Sea' ... It is understandable that the early Scandinavian voyagers, hearing the name *Kantalahti* [sic], should apply it, not only to the Gulf [i.e. Kandalaks Bay] but to all the neighbouring waters too.[20]

At the same time as weakening Jansson's general argument for the likelihood of a Norse etymology for *Bjarmar*, Ross thus increases the quantity of evidence pointing on the contrary to "proximate Bjarmian" derivation.

Scholars in the Norse field since the Second World War do not seem to have taken Jansson's and Ross's theories into account. Jan de Vries is content to repeat an explanation originally proposed by Max Förster and taken over from him by F. Holthausen to the effect that the Norse name of the Bjarmians is borrowed from Karelian by way of Lappish. The Bjarmians accordingly gave themselves their own name, which is etymologically related to that of the Permians; the mediation of Lappish is assumed in order to solve the problem of the voicing of

---

[19] Ross (1941), 202.
[20] Ross (1951/ii), 430. The Baltic Fennic etymology of *Gandvík* is already adumbrated in Ross's monograph (above, p. 32 note 4).

the initial consonant in the Norse form.[21] Commenting on this proposal in his special study of the route of borrowing, Ross writes that it

> ... would admittedly be an excellent suggestion if Ohthere's *Beormas* were the only Bjarmar we knew of ... Ohthere probably knew Lappish but not 'Bjarmian' ... and might thus well have taken his name for the Beormas from Turja-Lappish [i.e. the Lappish of the south coast of the Kola Peninsula]. But many of our Norse references are to the Dvina-Bjarmar and there seems no good reason for assuming that the Scandinavians took the name of the Karelian Bjarmar from the Lapps; it is far more probable that they took it from the Bjarmar themselves.[22]

The general drift of the argument here—as also in the case of the river-name *Vína*—makes it a little hard to understand why Ross ultimately opted for the contrary standpoint; the issue is not elaborated upon in his later contributions. In any case, it is unnecessary to resort to Lappish for an explanation of the voicing of initial *p*- in a Norse word assumed to have been borrowed from Karelian: the change can be quite sufficiently accounted for by the differences of articulation between the Germanic and Karelian consonant systems, the unaspirated *p*- of Old Northern Karelian being more likely to have been identified with ON. *b*- than with the aspirated ON. *p*-.[23]

Beormas/Bjarmar may, I think, safely be taken to be a Karelian loanword in Germanic and *Per(e)m'* to be a Karelian loanword in Russian. It remains to be shown how the Karelian

---

[21] J. de Vries, *Altnordisches etymologisches Wörterbuch* (1961), 39, following M. Förster, *Altenglisches Lesebuch*² (1921), 37 and F. Holthausen, *Altenglisches etymologisches Wörterbuch* (1934), 21; the etymology given by these latter authorities is described by de Vries as that "usually" accepted and Jansson's (but not Ross's) theory registered as an alternative.—Mediation of Lappish is, incidentally, invoked by Ross (1951/ii) to explain the initial consonant of Norse *Gandvík* (see above).

[22] Ross (as note 14), 8.

[23] Cf. Ekblom (1941-42), 138-9.—Ekblom, to whom Ross's work was apparently unknown, dismisses Jansson's Germanic etymology for *Bjarmaland* as "bold" (140); neither has Ross's alternative hypothesis won credence among Slavic philologists, as may be deduced e.g. from Julius Forssman's posthumously published *Skandinavische Spuren in der altrussischen Sprache und Dichtung* (Münchener Studien zur Sprachwissenschaft, Beiheft L, 1967), in which there is no mention of *Perem'* as a possible Scandinavian loanword.

word acquired its present ethno-geographical application in Russian, considering that modern scholars with the exception of Vasmer deny that there could have been any Old Permian settlement at the White Sea coast by the time of the first Norwegian *Bjarmaland* expeditions. The starting-point must be the type of culture which the Bjarmians established in the White Sea area. In spite of Ohthere's emphasis on Bjarmian occupation and (?) agriculture (cf. above, pp. 44-5, 53, 57), the region in which the Norsemen encountered the Bjarmians appears on archaeological evidence to have been only a secondary Karelian settlement. The Bjarmians of the White Sea were mainly roving groups, with home-lands farther south in the region of Lake Ladoga, and their chief errand in the Arctic wastes was the same as that of the Norwegians: to exploit the indigenous Lapps and to carry home the precious furs which constituted the chief source of the region's wealth.[24]

This insight makes it possible for us to understand some aspects of Ohthere's interview with Alfred rather better. He told the king that the Lapps of North Norway paid tribute in furs as well as in other wares (above, p. 20 lines 21-9), but when referring to the White Sea area he said that walrus tusks and hides were the main objects of commerce (*swiþost he for ðider ... for þæm horschwælum,* ibid. lines 1-2 = lines 5-6). In avoiding any explicit mention of furs from the White Sea area he was concealing an important trade secret from the English merchants[25] whose interests we may assume that the king was representing when he entertained his Norwegian guest.[26] There was no reason for Ohthere to share with the English his knowledge of an expanding source of imports; equally, there was no reason to admit that the *Bjarmar* actually offered formidable competition to the class of North Norwegian *entrepreneurs* to which he belonged. Hence his studied vagueness about his contacts with

---

[24] Tallgren (as note 15), *passim*; see also above, p. 46.

[25] Cf. Herbert Jankuhn, *Haithabu: ein Handelsplatz der Wikingerzeit*[4] (1963), 171-2.

[26] For a more general application of this interpretation to the geographical content of the OE. *Orosius* see Gustav Hübener, "König Alfreds Geografie |sic]", *Speculum* VI (1931), 428-34, at 430.

the *Bjarmar*: he had heard them tell many unverified stories (above, p. 18 lines 14-17 = lines 31-4) but did not care to sail past their boundaries (ibid. lines 11-12 = lines 28-9). This commercially shrewd Ohthere is an altogether more likely character than Whiting's "rugged individualist" who had fled to England from the centralizing policies and greed of Haraldr Hárfagri.[27]

The Bjarmians, then, had at least one thing in common with the Norwegians; both nations sought quick profits rather than a settled existence in the area of the White Sea. Such an interpretation is in full accord with the traditions of the sagas, which always represent the Norsemen as visiting *Bjarmaland* to plunder, not to seek a lasting home; and indeed the testimony of the sagas scarcely has much historical value other than as a general indication of the associations awakened by *Bjarmaland* in the minds of narrators. Admittedly there are genuine historical reminiscences in the references to the river Dvina and to the fur trade, e.g. in *Heimskringla, Hákonar saga gamla* and *Ǫrvar-Odds saga* (above, pp. 29-30, 33, 37); and the implied location of *Bjarmaland* somewhere to the East of the Gulf of Finland rather than in the area of the White Sea (above, pp. 32, 35, 38 note 17 [*Heiðreks saga*]; cf. p. 39 no. (xiii)(i)[28]) is perhaps a reflection of the fact that at least some Scandinavians knew about the connections of the Karelian Bjarmians with the Ladoga district. But it is equally clear that many of the extant saga

[27] Whiting (1945), esp. 223-6. Whiting's attempt to date Ohthere's visit to Alfred in relation to the battle of Hafrsfjǫrðr must be written off as a romantic failure. Nor can Kemp Malone's establishment of a *terminus ante quem* on the basis of Ohthere's reference to the extent of Danish rule in West Sweden be uncritically accepted, for it is uncertain whether Ohthere's voyage to Hedeby immediately preceded his voyage to England, or whether he would at all times have been informed about political events in South Norway (cf. Whiting 222 and reference there in note 21).

[28] For the possible relevance of this alternative location to the "two Biarmias" of Olaus Magnus cf. above, pp. 58-9. The more southerly *Bjarmaland* is presumably identical with Karelia (*Kirjálaland*) in *Egils saga*, ch. XIV (ed. Sigurður Nordal [Íslenzk fornrit II, 1933], 36 lines 14-16), where the sequence Namdalen-Jämtland-Hälsingland-Kvenland-Finland-Karelia obviously represents the viewpoint of a Norwegian looking eastwards across Sweden and the Baltic.

traditions are to a greater or lesser degree dependent on one another. Thus, *Heimskringla*'s anecdote of Þórir hundr's eleventh-century expedition to *Bjarmaland*, with its motifs of the collar around the neck of the god Jomali, the silver bowl and the precious metals buried in a mound,[29] displays affinities with *Bósa saga*, *Hálfs saga*, *Sturlaugs saga* and *Ǫrvar-Odds saga* (above, pp. 30-1, 34-6, 38). Similarly, the tradition in *Landnámabók* about Hjǫrr, who captures the Bjarmian princess Ljúfvina (p. 31), might be a variant of Saxo's story of the wooing of Thora (p. 39) and is of a type probably familiar to the redactors of *Bósa saga* and *Sturlaugs saga* (pp. 34-6). We have in other words to do with multiforms of the same core of Norse traditions connected with Bjarmaland, and a cumulative acceptance of their testimony is not to be contemplated. Nevertheless, the impression of *Bjarmaland* as an object of ruthless material exploitation is likely to be accurate enough.

This material exploitation is the key to the problem of the *Bjarmar*. The name does not signify an ethnic identity but rather a way of life: the Bjarmians were hunters and merchants who came from and returned to established settlements farther to the South, and who plundered the northern wastes and their wellnigh defenceless nomadic population for the natural resources in which the country abounded. In this sense Ohthere himself was at least a potential "Bjarmian"; but at the time when he and his fellow Norwegians reached the White Sea, the fur trade and related activities were dominated by Karelians from the vicinity of Lake Ladoga, and it was their name for themselves as a commercial group which the Norwegians borrowed—as a linguistic token, one might think, of professional jealousy and emulation. The Permians subsequently entered the region for the same purposes, and the Karelian group-appellation—when borrowed into Russian—came to be applied not only to the Karelian Bjarmians (as in *Kolo-Perem'*; see above, p. 72) but also to those Permians who had followed the Karelians' example in

---

[29] The word *Jomali* is, as shown by Ross, a Karelian loan, but the motifs of the idol and the votive mound are foreign to the religious usage of the Old Karelians and are perhaps derived from observation of the Lapps; cf. Tallgren (as note 15), 103 and 120.

pressing northwards to the White Sea coast. In later Russian usage, however, the word *Per(e)m'* was restricted to the Permians' primary area of settlement at the confluence of the Vym and Vychegda rivers and farther inland. The linguistic and historical hypotheses put forward here are to a great extent inspired by the work of the Finnish scholar Kustaa Vilkuna. In his brief but penetrating treatment of the Bjarmian problem published in 1956 Vilkuna draws attention to the Finnish dialect word *permi*, which was used of peripatetic merchants from Outer Karelia operating in groups throughout the length and breadth of Finland, North Sweden and Finnmark. As late as the beginning of the sixteenth century these people's commercial activity was so intense that it created problems for the Swedish central government, which was unable to obtain the quantity of fox skins which it required because the peasants of Österbotten preferred to trade with the Karelians. Ethnic descendants of these medieval Bjarmians were still to be found in 1876, when five Karelian families are recorded as living in isolation between the Russians and the Lapps at Välijärvi.[30] Finally, the participation of the (Zyrian) Permians in this distinctive variety of Arctic commerce was inspired by their contact with the Bolgars,[31] and the semantic development whereby *Perm'* came to be applied in Russian to the home-lands of the Permians is rendered plausible by the existence of the Finnish word-pair *Saksa* "Germany" ~ (non-literary) *saksa* "merchant".[32]

Vilkuna's construction is manifestly parallel to his treatment of the *Kvenir* (Ohthere's *Cwenas*), to which I refer in the last section of this Afterword. It can also be looked upon as an inversion of the theory launched by M. A. Castrén, who thought that the name "Bjarmians" for the Finnish inhabitants of the White Sea coast was inspired by the commercial fame of the Permians—rather

---

[30] Vilkuna (1956), 648. It may be inferred from the context that Vilkuna rejects the older etymologies connecting Russ. *Perm'* with Zyrian *parma* "wooded height" or Finn. *perämaa* "the land behind". Cf. Erkki Itkonen and Aulis J. Joki, *Suomen kielen etymologinen sanakirja* III (Lexica Societatis Fenno-Ugricae XII:3, 1962), s.v. *permi*; Jansson (as note 11), 46; Ekblom (1941-42), 139-40.
[31] Vilkuna (1956), 649; cf. Tallgren (as note 15), 108.
[32] Vilkuna (1956), 650.

than *vice versa*.³³ Castrén's theory was already undermined by the work of Kuznetsov and others, who proved that the concept of a rich and powerful Old Permian nation was based on fancy rather than fact. It is, however, an interesting sidelight on twentieth-century Soviet historiography that the "Permian myth" was resuscitated by the nationalistic Communist leaders of the autonomous Komi *oblast* in the 1920s, only to be suppressed along with other manifestations of deviationism after the incorporation of the *oblast* in the northern section of the RSFSR in 1929. In this connection it is a mere curiosity, though a regrettable one, that the latest reported Russian contribution on *Bjarmaland*, published by A. L. Nikitin in 1976, attempts to show that there was no *Bjarmaland* located near the White Sea and that the *Bjarmar* were Celts (!) dwelling in the South-East Baltic.³⁴

I have referred to Ohthere as "at least a potential 'Bjarmian' " (above, p. 77), and argued that his role at Alfred's court should be given a commercial interpretation. It seems highly unlikely to me that his fame would have been so great as to earn him the status of hero in an oral saga; yet this notion has been canvassed as recently as 1946 in a book by Nora K. Chadwick. Ohthere is here identified with Qrvar-Oddr, whose dealings with the Viking Skolli in England are chronologically equated with Ohthere's arrival in that country on the journey which brought him to King Alfred. The northern voyages of Ohthere/Oddr are seen as frustrated searches for a North-East Passage to the Orient; Ohthere's report to King Alfred may be "an epitome of an Anglo-Saxon version" of the earlier part of *Qrvar-Odds saga*.³⁵

---

³³ Cf. Jansson (as note 11), 43 and references there given.
³⁴ See Stang (1978). This writer's unpublished thesis on "Bjarmene—deres identitet, eksistensgrunnlag og forbindelser med andre folkeslag . . ." (Oslo University: Department of History, 1977 [cf. Stang (1978), 300 note 1]) has not been available to me.
³⁵ "The Scandinavian Background: *Oddr Víthförli (Örvar-Oddr)*", in Chadwick (1946), 145-74, at 149-50 and 169-74.—It should be said that the identification of Ohthere with Qrvar-Oddr was not Nora Chadwick's invention: it goes back to Gustav Storm and R. C. Boer (cf. the latter's paper "Über die Qrvar-Odds saga", *Arkiv för nordisk filologi* VIII [1892], 97-139, at 102-5 and 139), though the inspiration of these scholars is not acknowledged in her book.

These fantastic speculations have not, as far as I know, left any impression on Norse or Anglo-Saxon studies in the last generation. The more usual and pragmatic view of Ohthere and his report has stimulated interest in the strictly geographical as well as the ethnographic and historical aspects of the text. Much learned ink has been spilt on the possibility of "shifted orientation" as an explanation of the bearings mentioned in the Ohthere interpolation and in other topographical passages in the OE. *Orosius*. The suspicion that the text conceals a systematic deflection of the points of the compass *vis à vis* True North was first voiced by Henrik Gabriel Porthan in 1800, and twentieth-century proponents of the deflection theory—with varieties of emphasis and interpretation—have included Lauritz Weibull, Kemp Malone and Richard Ekblom.[36] Since the Second World War, however, the deflection theory has yielded to more cautious and at the same time more historically relevant readings of the passages in question. Where Malone, for example, reckoned with a 45° easterly deflection of certain compass bearings, and Ekblom with a 60° deflection in bearings expressed according to what he thought was a specifically "Old Scandinavian" orientation, Alvar Ellegård has denied that the texts can be read literally and has emphasized the "itinerary" principle as a fundamental concept in medieval geographical description. Directions given are often indicative of the "ultimate" orientation of the journey, i.e. of the final destination as conceived in relation to the point of departure.[37] Extreme cases of deviation can be due to "name" orientation, as when an Icelander coming from the South-East speaks of himself as travelling south to Reykjavík, because Reykjavík, the capital city, is always thought of as

---

[36] Cf. Malone (reference above, p. 12); Ekblom (1941-42); and other works quoted in Ellegård (1954-55), 1 notes 1-4.—Porthan's treatise on the *Orosius*, which was Finland's first contribution to the study of English (or any other modern language outside the Nordic and Finno-Ugric families), is described in Enkvist (1956-57).

[37] Ellegård (1954-55); cf. Ekblom (1960; posthumously printed) and Ellegård (1960).

situated in the southern part of the island.³⁸ A variant of this more recent school of thought is the solution offered by William C. Stokoe for the notorious crux in Ohthere's account of the route south from *Halgoland* to *Sciringes heal*: when Ohthere speaks of having first *Iraland* and then England to starboard, he means that the points of departure for the ocean passage to these destinations are reached in the given order.³⁹ More immediately relevant to Ohthere's *Bjarmaland* voyage is Alan Binns's attempt to deal with the orientation problem by reference to the employment of dead reckoning.⁴⁰ All these differences of scholarly opinion serve to emphasize the desirability of caution in drawing conclusions from details in the transmitted text.

At the conclusion of his report on the White Sea area Ohthere gives a description of his own country, Norway. Among other things he remarks that *Cwenaland* runs parallel to the northern part of Norway on the other side of the mountains which demarcate the East Norwegian frontier (above, p. 22 lines 9-12). He adds that the *Cwenas* carry their boats overland to the lakes in the mountains, thus utilizing the inland waterways to mount attacks on the Norwegians (ibid. lines 12-16). This passage is not treated in Ross's monograph (cf. above, p. 24 note 4), but he has discussed it in an investigation reported in Finnish in 1953 and in English in the following year. His hypothesis is that the portage route referred to by Ohthere leads from the eastern end of Torne träsk (in the extreme North of modern Sweden) across the watershed between lakes Vuosko and Leine and down

---

³⁸ For Icelandic orientation see Stefán Einarsson, "Terms of direction in Modern Icelandic", *Scandinavian Studies presented to George T. Flom* . . . (Illinois Studies in Language and Literature XXIX:1, 1942), 37-48; idem, "Terms of direction in Old Icelandic", *JEGP* XLIII (1944), 265-85; Einar Haugen, "The semantics of Icelandic orientation", *Word* XIII (1957), 447-60; and Tryggve Sköld, "Isländska väderstreck", *Scripta Islandica* XVI (1966 *for* 1965), 1-61.
³⁹ W. C. Stokoe, Jr., "On Ohthere's *steorbord*", *Speculum* XXXII (1957), 299-306. For earlier interpretations of *Iraland* (including the equation of the name with Iceland) see references in Stokoe, 299 note 3; Iceland is also supported by Ellegård (1954-55), 6 note 5 and by Björn Þorsteinsson, "Íraland = Ísland?", *Tímarit Máls og menningar* XXVI (1965), 72-81.
⁴⁰ Binns (1961), 50-1.

the river system which flows into Malangen Fjord.⁴¹ The boats used were perhaps like the portable Lapp boat described in Linnæus' *Iter lapponicum* (1732); as to the identity of the *Cwenas*, they were the Finnish *kainulaiset*, called *Kvenir* in Old Norse sources. These *Kvenir* are a people whose name and history have been much debated by Finnish historians. They are familiar to students of the sagas from the story of Þórólfr Kveld-Úlfsson in *Egils saga*, who allied himself briefly with the *Kvenir* and their king Faravið in a campaign against the Karelians.⁴² They seem to have been a para-military organisation which hunted, traded and plundered in an area extending from the North Baltic to Lapland and Finnmark. Kustaa Vilkuna has argued that their Finnish name is related to the word *kainu(t), kainus*, which occurs in South-West Finnish dialects as an appellation for part of an ancient sledge construction, the significant feature of the *kainut* being that it was shaped somewhat like a club. The conclusion arrived at—by means of reasoning too complex to be repeated here—is that the leader of a group of *Kvenir* like "King" Faravið in *Egils saga* carried a stave called **kainut* as a symbol of his authority, and that the word *kainulaiset* is a secondary formation referring to the members of a group which functioned under such a leader.⁴³ The *Kvenir* would thus be men from South-West Finland engaged in activities analogous to those of the Karelian Bjarmians, whose home-lands and main area of operations in the Arctic lay farther to the East than those of the *Kvenir*. All of this makes good sense of the tradition preserved in *Egils saga*, chs. XIV and XVII, where we find the *Kvenir* inviting Norsemen to cooperate with them on an *ad hoc* basis against the rival Karelians. It is probable, though not entirely clear from the context, that the *Kylfingar* referred to in ch. X of the saga are identical with the *Kvenir*; *Kylfingar* is usually held to be an

---

⁴¹ A. S. C. Ross, "Kainulaisten kulkureitti hyökkäysretkillä norjalaisten kimppuun", in *Uuden Suomen Viikkolehti*, 20.12.1953; cf. Ross (1954).
⁴² *Egils saga* (1933), 35-7 and 41 (chs. XIV and XVII). Cf. the paraphrase and discussion in Whiting (1945).
⁴³ K. Vilkuna, *Kainuu-Kvenland, missä ja mikä?* (1957). Swedish version with additions: Vilkuna (1969).

umlaut-formation from the root seen in ON. *kolfr* "(rounded) stem, bolt, etc." and could thus be a translation-loan from the old Finnish name for the *Kvenir*. If, on the other hand, *Kylfingar* is a translation of the ethnic designation for the Vots, the question would arise whether not only Finns and Karelians but also other Baltic Fennic elements were to be encountered in the wilds of Finnmark.[44]

Ohthere's report of periodic hostilities between Norwegians and *Kvenir* is doubtless true; but the two peoples were quite capable of making common cause against a competitor in the ongoing commercial struggle for control of the Arctic hinterland. In the eyes of a North Norwegian merchant of the second half of the ninth century the *Bjarmar* were very much a force to be reckoned with, and Ohthere—as he indeed tells us— was careful to respect their territorial limits on the White Sea.[45]

SELECT BIBLIOGRAPHY AND ABBREVIATED REFERENCES

For the convenience of the reader I here provide a select list of publications relevant to the study of Ohthere's northern voyage which have appeared since Professor Ross published his monograph; items included in the sequence of *Ohtheriana*

[44] For the equation *Kylfingar* (*Egils saga* [1933], 27-8) = *Kvenir* see Vilkuna (1969), 112, where the proper name *Faravið* is also explained as a translation-loan (cf. older Finn. *Kaukamoinen*). The suggestion that *Kylfingar* translates the name of the Vots is to be found in B. Briem's "Kylfingar", *Acta Philologica Scandinavica* IV (1929-30), 40-8; cf. however above, p. 49 note 26 and p. 55. The Vots (Vatja, most recently located near Leningrad, cf. map) became extinct during the Second World War.—It may be noted that an explanation of *Kylfingar* on precisely the same lines as Vilkuna's treatment of *Kvenir/kainulaiset* was already offered by Ad. Stender-Petersen, "Zur bedeutungsgeschichte des wortes altnord. *kylfingr*, altruss. *kolb'ag*", *Acta Philologica Scandinavica* VII (1932-33), 181-92, reprinted in Stender-Petersen, "Die Väringer und Kylfinger", *Varangica* (1953), 89-113, at 99-111. This Danish study is nowhere quoted in the bibliographical apparatus to Vilkuna (1969).

[45] For a variety of suggestions and assistance with points of detail I have to thank Peter Foote (London), Michael Larsen and Bjarne Nørretranders (Copenhagen) and Desmond Slay (Aberystwyth).

initiated by Ross after the Second World War are explicitly identified in those cases where their membership of the sequence does not appear from the published title.

Binns, A. L. "Ohtheriana VI: Ohthere's northern voyage", *English and Germanic Studies* VII (1961), 43-52. BINNS (1961)

Brewer, D. S. "Sixteenth, seventeenth and eighteenth century references to the Voyage of Ohthere (Ohtheriana IV)", *Anglia* LXXI (1952-53), 202-11.

Chadwick, Nora K. *The Beginnings of Russian History: An Enquiry into Sources*, Cambridge 1946. CHADWICK (1946)

Ekblom, Richard. "Alfred the Great as Geographer", *A Philological Miscellany presented to Eilert Ekwall* I = *Studia Neophilologica* XIV (1941-42), 115-44. EKBLOM (1941-42)

Ekblom, Richard. "King Alfred, Ohthere and Wulfstan: Reply to a Critique", *Studia Neophilologica* XXXII (1960), 3-13. EKBLOM (1960)

Ellegård, Alvar. "De gamla nordbornas väderstrecksuppfattning" [with English summary: "The System of Orientation among the Old Scandinavians"], *Lychnos* 1954-55, 1-20. ELLEGÅRD (1954-55)

Ellegård, Alvar. "The Old Scandinavian System of Orientation", *Studia Neophilologica* XXXII (1960), 241-8. ELLEGÅRD (1960)

Enkvist, Nils Erik. "Porthans 'Försök at uplysa Konung Ælfreds Geographiska Beskrifning öfver den Europeiska Norden'", *Åbo Akademi. Årsskrift* XLI (1956-57), 1-20 [English summary = *Ohtheriana* VII]. ENKVIST (1956-57)

Haavio, Martti. *Bjarmien vallan kukoistus ja tuho* [The Rise and Fall of Bjarmian Power], Porvoo/Helsinki 1965.

Johansen, Paul. "Kylfinger", *Kulturhistorisk leksikon for nordisk middelalder* IX (1964), 602-4.

Kirkinen, Eikki [sic]. "La Laponie, objet des rivalités au moyen âge et au début des âges modernes", *Inter-Nord* XI (1970), 125-35.

Koutaissoff, E. "Ohtheriana I: Kuznetsov on Biarmia", *English and Germanic Studies* II (1948-49), 20-33. KOUTAISSOFF (1948-49)

Labuda, Gerard. "Chorografia Orozjusza w anglosaskim przekładzie króla Alfreda" [Orosius' Chorography in King Alfred's Anglo-Saxon Translation], *Źródła skandynawskie i anglosaskie do dziejów słowiańszczyzny* [Scandinavian and Anglo-Saxon Sources of Slavic History] (Fontes origines Polonorum illustrantes, Fontes septentrionales I), Warsaw 1961, 5-118.

Luukko, Armas. "Kväner", *Kulturhistorisk leksikon for nordisk middelalder* IX (1964), 599-602.

Ross, Alan S. C. "The Name of the Northern Dvina", *Modern Language Quarterly* II (1941), 199-202. Ross (1941)

Ross, Alan S. C. "Ohtheriana II: Tatishchev's *Byarma*", appendix to E. Koutaissoff, "Tatishchev's 'Joachim Chronicle'", *University of Birmingham Historical Journal* III: 1 (1951), 52-63, at 61-3. Ross (1951/i)

Ross, Alan S. C. "The place-name Kandalaksha", *Troisième congrès international de toponymie et d'anthroponymie*, ed. H. Draye and O. Jodogne, II-III: *Actes et mémoires*, Louvain 1951, 429-32 [*Ohtheriana* III]. Ross (1951/ii)

Ross, Alan S. C. "Ohthere's 'Cwenas and Lakes'", *Geographical Journal* CXX (1954), 337-45 [*Ohtheriana* V]. Ross (1954)

Stang, Håkon. "'Biarmia' i sovjetisk historiografi", *(Norsk) Historisk tidsskrift* 1978, 300-10. STANG (1978)

Vilkuna, Kustaa. "Bjarmer och Bjarmaland", *Kulturhistorisk leksikon for nordisk middelalder* I (1956), 647-51. VILKUNA (1956)

Vilkuna, Kustaa. *Kainuu-Kvänland: ett finsk-norsk-svenskt problem* (Acta Academiae regiae Gustavi Adolphi XLVI), Uppsala 1969. VILKUNA (1969)

Whiting, B. J. "Óhthere (Óttar) and *Egils saga*", *Philological Quarterly* XXIV (1945), 218-26. WHITING (1945)

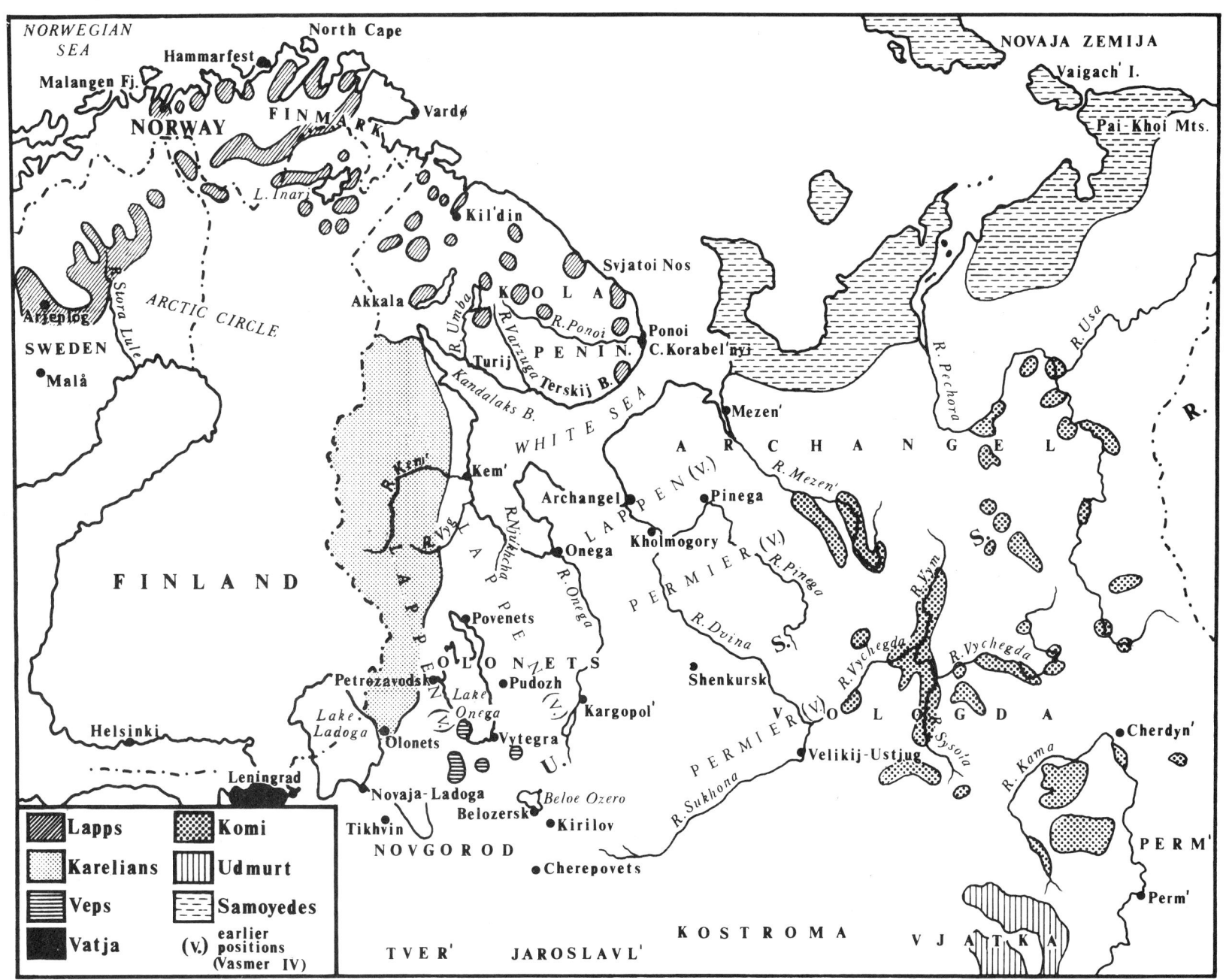